F

Also by
Natasha Esch

Wilhelmina's
World of
Child Modeling

Wilhelmina's
Modeling &
Acting Dictionary

THE WILHELMINA GUIDE TO MODELING

Natasha Esch
with C. L. Walker

Fireside
Published by Simon & Schuster

FIRESIDE

Rockefeller Center

1230 Avenue of the Americas

New York, NY 10020

FIRESIDE and colophon are registered trademarks of Simon & Schuster Inc.

DESIGNED BY BARBARA MARKS

Manufactured in the United States of America

10   9   8   7   6

Library of Congress Cataloging-in-Publication Data

Esch, Natasha, date.

The Wilhelmina guide to modeling / Natasha Esch with C. L. Walker.

p.   cm.

1. Models (Persons)—Vocational guidance.   I. Walker, C. L.

(Christine L.)

HD6073.M77E83   1996

746.92—dc20   96-12253   CIP

ISBN 0-684-81491-9
ISBN: 978-0-684-81491-9

Acknowledgments

Special thanks to: Jay Alexander, Cynthia Bailey, Nancy Bauer, Michael Bergin, Maria DiAngelis, Garren, Rebecca Gayheart, Rachel Goldstein, David Grilli, Michael Guy, Jill Hunter, Beverly Johnson, Kevin Jones, Judy Linton, Larry Matlaw, Donna Miranda, Alexandra Monachev, Angela Neil, Rhonda Niles, Doug Ordway, Sean Patterson, Chris Petrock, PMK, Angela Shelton, Tomiko, Mark Vanderloo, Aric Webb, Kathy Williams, Ziggi, and all the models and staff at Wilhelmina Models for their help and encouragement.

To Wilhelmina,
without whom
this book would
not have been
possible and
who has paved
the way for
countless young
adults to pursue
their dreams in
modeling.

Contents

Foreword

Rebecca Gayheart

"Forget it, Rebecca. You'll never be a model. You're too short!" Those were the words I heard over and over again whenever I mentioned the possibility of modeling.

Even the most determined, willful, headstrong eighteen-year-old needs someone on her side. Natasha Esch became that person. She saw something in me that others missed. She encouraged me to emphasize my strengths—my energy, spontaneity, personality and professionalism. While Natasha worked at a small agency called Faces during her summers off from college, we learned the business together. We were both dedicated and ambitious. She believed in me. And when she became director of Wilhelmina Models, Inc., she convinced me to sign with her.

In *The Wilhelmina Guide to Modeling*, Natasha shares her gifts for motivating and inspiring young people to make the most of their talents. She understands what a huge and daunting place the world of modeling might appear to be to the uninitiated newcomer. Let her guide you through that world—so you can make your chances of suc-cess the best they can be. Meet the industry professionals behind the supermodels, and learn about the hard work behind all that glamor. Avoid the pitfalls and explore the highlights of this exciting career!

I've seen so many models make mistakes at the beginning of their careers that could easily have been avoided had they been given a little guidance and information. This book can save you money and valuable time. Use it to learn as much as you can about your business. Have faith in yourself and in your potential. Go all out. Give it 100 percent! And, Good Luck!

Introduction

Natasha Esch

When I was first intro-
duced to the exciting world of
modeling, I took it
upon myself to learn everything I
possibly could about the business.
A serious student, I quizzed every
industry expert I met: agents, photographers, art directors, designers,
business people, and the models
themselves. I searched the shelves
of libraries and bookstores for
books about the fashion industry,
books about photography, hair
and makeup, and books about
modeling. And I found clear com-
prehensive guides in all of these
areas—except one. Not one major
industry professional had assem-
bled an elementary guide designed
to educate the perspective model on
the basics of the industry. No wonder so many young models find
themselves living by their wits at
the beginning of their careers. A
model has her pick of diet and fitness books, historical perspectives
on fashion, and volumes of industry
gossip, but no hands-on guide that
clearly defines the elements I now
know to be imperative for success
in the complex world of modeling.

To fill this gap, I have designed a
no-nonsense guide for anyone
interested in becoming a model. In
my function as president of Wilhelmina Models, I am asked questions by models every day. These
questions have given me greater
insight into the concerns of the
beginning model. They have helped
this book evolve and gain dimen-
sion. I must thank the models for
their openness and candor. I have
always tried to answer their questions as empathetically and defini-
tively as possible. When I did not
have the answer, I said so, and did
more research. I hope this book
takes that extra step in addressing
all those questions.

The world of modeling is ever-
changing. This makes it a very
exciting place to be. Most recently,
male models have been gaining the
recognition they deserve. Since Wilhelmina Models has become a
leader in this area of the industry, I
am proud to have devoted a substantial portion of the book to the
growing opportunities for men.

Now, I know that you are inun-
dated with the gossip and scandal
of all the supermodels. It's glamorous and entertaining stuff, and
easily found on newsstands everywhere. If you want to read more
about it, I would suggest sources

other than this book. But, if you want to take some clear-cut steps to increase your chances of success in the industry—if you want a head start, take advantage of all the advice collected from experts in every part of the modeling industry. Read on. You've hit the jackpot.

A successful businessman once told me, "The ability to have the most accurate information is the key to success in business." This book will give you precisely that information. Study it and you will stand a much better chance of realizing your dream of becoming a model. And to all of you who read this book, enjoy it, and good luck in the pursuit of your dreams, wherever they may take you.

Now, take a good long look at yourself in the mirror. **You are your product**—your face, your body and mind, your personality, enthusiasm, dedication and commitment. Only you can build a career for yourself. Sure, you'll need the guidance and expertise of agents and industry professionals, but in the end, it'll be up to you.

Contrary to popular opinion, supermodels, and the fame, power and fortunes they command, are not created overnight. They don't just happen. They are, however, *created.* But the new model is fast becoming the master of her destiny, not the pawn of an industry. Cindy Crawford, supermodel, television host, fitness expert, actress, businesswoman and multimillionaire, is the perfect example. Even though she may consult closely with expert advisers, Cindy always has final say. At the same time, Cindy is always professional—punctual, cooperative and willing to work hard to get the job done.

Models are getting smarter and, consequently, more powerful and successful every day—some, like Cindy, are even heading up their own empires. They're smart about their career plans, their health, their investments. And they're smart about *business.*

That's what this book is all about—helping a new generation of models get serious and get smart. The information you need to become a successful model is contained in these pages; a wealth of experience from established professionals combined with the fresh perspectives of the young, smart and very serious newcomers who are in a position to shape the future of the industry. This book will give you the insight to make the most of your strengths. It will give you the power to *invent yourself.* Take that power! There are beautiful girls and guys everywhere. Knowledge will give you the confidence to make better choices, and these choices are key to your success.

In the beginning, models were not so powerful. Some worked as artists' models, illustrators' muses, designers' dress forms. Their careers were shaped by the artists who chose them. They accepted as payment whatever they were given and were discarded when an artist tired of them or found a fresh replacement. Some were treated well—most were not. They had no agent to guide them, to demand that they be paid fairly (or at all), to plan a career, to see that they reached their full potential and power as models and businesspeople. Today, some male models rival female supermodels in fame, power and opportunities, but until just a few years ago, male print models were still being employed primarily as background figures or props for their higher profile female counterparts.

In New York, in 1925, there was one modeling agency—run by John Robert Powers. You're familiar with the name because of the network of schools that span the country. Well, the first "Powers girls" earned about $20 a week. By 1935, a number of agents were managing the careers of about two hundred working models who commanded $25 to $75 per week. The half dozen "supermodels" of the day earned about $100 per week! By contrast, today's supermodels, with cosmetics contracts and product endorsements, make *several million dollars a year.* And if Lauren Hutton and Cheryl Tiegs are examples, a top model's career can span decades. Furthermore, once established, models are expanding their talents in a wide variety of directions: as actors, television hosts, novelists, restaurateurs, photographers, singers and filmmakers. The opportunities are endless.

So what does it take to become successful? It takes commitment, a good aptitude for business, an eagerness to work hard, as well as being "exceptionally beautiful." But just try to define the "exceptionally beautiful" part. You can't. At one time, a female print model had to be 5'8" or taller, a size 6–8, and blond to have any hope of becoming a top model. The range of acceptable "looks" is far greater today. Even the height requirement is, on occasion, set aside. Consider supermodel Kate Moss and Noxzema girl Rebecca Gayheart, both measuring in at under 5'7".

Rebecca is the perfect example of the potential of focused conviction and attitude. She came to New York from Kentucky at fifteen, determined to make a career with Wilhelmina Models. But she's only 5'6". So she had to fight hard against that. Granted, she is a beautiful girl. Her clients will tell you that she is also vibrant, enthusiastic and a joy to work with.

FOR HEALTHY LOOKING SKIN

Your face, how you take care of it says a lot about you.

So you use Noxzema every time you wash.

It's better than soap. Dissolves oil while it conditions. For skin that's soft, smooth.

Noxzema. And nothing less.

Noxzema

Photo: Peggy Sirota/Noxzema

Rebecca's energy, personality and charisma more than make up for any lack in height. Clients would rather work with a girl like Rebecca than a 5'9" girl who might be uncooperative. Rebecca has also always been keenly oriented toward her goals and very serious about her career. So you can be a little bit unusual, an individual, and still pull it all together, work hard and become very successful in this industry.

People talk about trends in the fashion industry, such as the trend toward smaller, waiflike models being replaced by fuller figured, more glamorous types—but look around you. The so-called waifs like Kate Moss haven't disappeared. They've just reinvented themselves. These girls are professionals. They adapt to the needs of the industry, and their agents market them accordingly. In photographs, Christy Turlington appeared fragile and doll-like during the years of the "waif." She epitomized movie-star glamor when that look "came back." And when a strong, fit, earthy type is in, *she is just that.* That's why she's among the handful of supermodels who land valuable contracts and major advertising campaigns and grace magazine covers year after year.

These models are smart, versatile and accomplished businesspeople. It is important that a model develop not only a marketable look but the maturity not to get caught up in the glamor, fun and games of the business. At the same time, a model must develop professionalism and business acumen. No one expects a fifteen-year-old to have the experience of a crack business-woman. That's why there are agents to guide fledgling careers. But eventually a model will have to make some choices, and that's often when careers are made or broken.

Yes, there are models who do the work, who make their $1500 per day rate, and some of them are very smart, and some less so. But in order to be at the top, you have to have a sharp eye for business.

1 GETTING
STARTED

Generally, your chances of becoming successful as a female print model are best if you are between 5'9" and 5'11", a dress size 6–8, with long slender limbs, a long graceful neck and a beautiful face with even features.

Most models maintain a disciplined exercise routine. There are some notable exceptions among the female ranks, however. A few girls with unbelievable figures claim never to have exercised at all! Procedures such as breast enlargement, tummy and thigh liposuction and even calf implants can dramatically alter the shape of a woman's body. Some models have even gone so far as to have ribs removed to make their waists smaller. But some of these "jobs" are rather obvious looking. I'm sure examples come to mind. Plastic surgery is not recommended for models, male or female. The results are unpredictable and often permanent. Many of the procedures are expensive and dangerous. *There is always risk involved:* the risk of infection and scarring. Even the risks posed by general anesthesia must be considered. No career is worth risking your life—if you don't have the prerequisites, don't try to create them.

A model, male or female, with the right proportions, who is healthy, exercises and maintains a balanced diet will be in ideal form for assignments. There are few fig-

Physical Requirements

ure problems that can't be corrected by diet and exercise if the basic body proportions are within the range required for modeling. Even when a girl is shorter than 5'9", with measurements less than the typical bust 34, waist 24, hips 34, she may find work as a beauty model, as a petite model, in the smaller markets, or in Japan. We've already noted that a few exceptionally beautiful girls have done well as models in the major markets even though they are smaller in stature than the usual requisite. Bigger girls can explore the growing plus size market. A number of major New York agencies have divisions for larger size models, including Wilhelmina Models and Ford Models.

Of course, there's work for all shapes and sizes in commercial print and television. All the major American markets have agencies that handle talented professionals interested in pursuing careers in these areas.

A minimum exercise routine for the busy model consists of twenty minutes of sustained aerobic exercise (dance, step classes, bicycling, in-line skating, swimming) three times a week. This will maintain the all-round healthy, toned look that is most in demand in all markets.

Always consult your physician before beginning any new exercise routine.

Schools and Contests

While modeling schools are not a necessary step for the beginning model, some of them do bring in agents of reputation to review their graduating students. Occasionally, a promising student is invited to New York to test with a prominent agency. But that same individual would likely attract an agent's attention by simply sending in a snapshot or by entering one of the contests sponsored each year by the major agencies—and at considerably less expense than the cost of attending a modeling school.

The contests sponsored by legitimate agencies are certainly a good way to get noticed. Every year, the winners and finalists in

Photo: Barton Jahncke

model searches are groomed by major agencies and find themselves in great demand as new faces in the industry. Some of them, like Cindy Crawford and Stephanie Seymour, have gone on to become supermodels. Wilhelmina Models sponsors a nationwide model search every year. The grand prize is a $100,000 modeling contract. If you would like to enter this year's contest just fill out the application at the back of the book and mail it to us at Wilhelmina Models in New York.

not be asked for funds up front. These promotional expenses will be deducted from future paychecks.

Sean Patterson, an agent in the Wilhelmina Men's Division, offers some additional words of caution for the aspiring model.

Model Beware

The importance of securing legitimate, responsible representation cannot be emphasized enough. **Agents who ask you for money up front—whether it be for a photo session, composite, head sheet or any other promotional tool—should be avoided.** A reputable agent will not ask you for money until you are making money— booking work as a result of contacts the agency has made for you. That is the time to invest in a composite and in the agency book and head sheet. Even then you will probably

"If there was one thing I could change about the industry it would be to institute a more rigid policing of the model conventions that are being held all over the country. You see, the people who run these hotel conventions charge registration and attendance fees anywhere from $300 to $1500 to young guys and girls who want to be models. And what they do is, they invite one agent from this agency and one agent from that agency, and they offer these agents an all-expenses-paid trip to the host city—give them a stipend of $150–$200 for the day. It's a free trip for these agents. Now the advertisements go up—ads luring aspiring models by saying that there will be in attendance agents from Wilhelmina, Elite, Ford—European agencies too. So these young people, mostly girls, pay these fees to the conventioneers, who clean up. And there is usually no process of preselection. Anybody, regardless of ability or potential, can attend, if they pay the fee."

As somebody who grew up not having a lot of money, I know what it feels like to put pressure on your parents to come up with the money for something that they really can't afford. So I bet that at most of these conventions at least a segment of the group attending are spending money they don't have to spend, money that could be invested, say, in school tuition. At the same time, many of these young people don't have a chance of ever becoming a successful model or a model at all. So it becomes a total waste. Furthermore, contacts made at conventions can lead to further rip-offs—out-of-work photographers flock to these conventions and approach young hopefuls: "Let's do a test on you. Let's spend $300 to $500 to start you off with a portfolio of professional pictures!" And it is generating huge amounts of cash for people who aren't going to do anything for these young women's and men's careers. This sort of setup does not belong in the modeling industry. It serves no purpose to the industry. Rather, it is an industry unto itself, one that preys on teenagers hoping to become models and parents who want to please them. I guess I'm asking for a little more care, a little more honesty.

If you really want to be a model and give it a shot, contact an agency in your hometown, or a major agency in a larger city, and *send snapshots.*

A Model's First Photographs

Take Sean's advice. Don't waste money on so-called professional photographs. Usually they will not be of a standard acceptable to a reputable agency. The quality of pictures in model portfolios is extremely high. Even basic test shots are the result of carefully planned sessions. The photographer is usually an experienced professional who has worked in editorial print. Expert makeup artists, hairstylists and clothing stylists are brought in to make every element of the test work. The photographs resulting from a test shoot are only as strong as their weakest link. Competitive industry professionals cannot afford to waste time and money by leaving any element of the shoot to chance. Furthermore, when a test is arranged by an agency, you will usually not be asked to contribute any photo fee. At most, you may be asked to help cover the cost of film and processing (less than $100 at most sittings).

It is unlikely that a photographer who is asking you to pay for pictures will be capable of bringing the best of these elements together. So your pictures will appear semiprofessional, and that will make you look bad to a prospective agency. In their view, it is better for you not to have worked at all—**to be a fresh discovery**—than to have worked with less than exceptional people. So just send us a couple of snapshots. They really do afford you your best chance. I must emphasize that under no circumstances should you be convinced that getting expensive photos will heighten your chances of being noticed by an agent. Agents have a terrific eye for determining potential from a snapshot. After all, it's their job.

Agents want to see sharp snapshots of you looking as natural as possible. A close-in photograph of your face, without makeup, and a full-length shot, preferably in a bathing suit, are ideal. Natural light is the most flattering. Have a parent or friend take your picture outside, early in the morning or just before the sun sets. At these times, when the sun is low in the sky, the light creates soft, flattering skin tones.

Once you have two sharp snaps of yourself, you're ready to contact the agencies.

Natasha's Snapshot Guidelines—

Bad

Too dark
(underexposed)

Too light
(overexposed)

Hair covering face

Poor composition
(subject too distant)

Too much makeup

Photo: G. Bruckheimer

The Dos and Don'ts of Snapshots

Good

Correctly exposed

Correct composition

Natural look

Photo: G. Bruckheimer

Photo: G. Bruckheimer

Photo: G. Bruckheimer

In a notebook, make a list of the agencies in your area that you wish to contact. Many models begin their careers in their hometown markets. Compile a second list of the agencies you wish to contact in the major markets: New York, Los

Contacting the Agencies

Angeles, Chicago, and Miami. Telephone the agents in your area and ask if they hold **open calls** for new models. You may be asked your age, height and weight. Most agencies will see young women between the ages of fifteen and twenty, with a minimum height of 5'9". If you do not meet the requirements for the open call, send snapshots. Open calls are held each week, giving aspiring models the chance to interview with an agency. If you arrive at an open call and are too short or too old, you will be dismissed immediately. If you do meet the requirements and plan to attend an open call, bring snapshots with you. Print your name, date of birth and phone number, along with your height and measurements, on a sticker and place it on the back of

each photograph. Don't wear makeup. Wear your hair in a simple style, away from your face, and dress in simple form-fitting clothing. When you do talk to an agent, be yourself. Indicate that you want to model and plan to make a serious commitment to your work—that you are cooperative, energetic and determined to work hard.

How is a model chosen by an agent? Judy Linton, director of the Women's Division at Wilhelmina, explains what happens when the "right" girl walks into the agency. "It's like falling in love," she says. "You can't pinpoint when it's going to happen. It just happens. You get a feeling. The girl will be beautiful, and her expression will portray a sense of openness and responsibility. It doesn't matter the color of the eyes as long as they're expressive, evenly spaced. Fuller lips are preferred to thinner but, again, it's an overall experience. I can see a blond girl with big blue eyes, but then the nose is not quite right with the rest of the face. But when everything comes together, you know it."

Kevin Jones, agent in Wilhelmina's W2 Division, elaborates. "There's a connection. We look for beautiful eyes, beautiful skin, a great attitude. There are some girls who tend to be very beautiful but are very dead behind it all. Being a little more extroverted helps. This is not a business for anybody who wants to be shy. It's just not that kind of business. You have to go after what you want. The modeling game is all about knowing, being social, being out there."

If an agency does not see models on open calls, you will probably be asked to send snapshots of yourself. Send one head shot and one full length photo with a simple covering letter and a self-addressed stamped envelope for the agent's reply and the return of your photographs. Study the following sample covering letter.

Your name
Street address
City, State, Zip code

Date

Name of Contact at Agency
Agency name
Street address
City, State, Zip code

Dear Mr./Ms. _____

Enclosed are several snapshots and an SASE for your reply and for the return of the pictures. I am prepared to make the necessary arrangements to meet with you at your convenience should you show interest in representing me. Thank you very much for your consideration.

My personal statistics are as follows:

Age and date of birth:
Height:
Size:
Hair color:
Eye color:
Special Talents: (i.e., sports, dance, musical instruments, swimming, etc.)

Sincerely,
Your name
Phone number

Sample Covering Letter

You may be one of the lucky few who are "discovered" at an open call. If an agent is interested in you, they will ask you to work with them for a trial period, during which your potential as a model will be assessed. You will meet photographers and participate in test photo sessions.

tographs or may suggest that you explore opportunities locally to gain some experience before applying again. It's a good idea to apply to several agencies. You may not fit the "look" of a particular agency but may be right for another. Remember that the choice of models is a subjective one. Many famous models were rejected on their first

The Agency Response

If an agency is interested in the pictures you've sent, they will telephone or write to arrange a personal interview. These interviews usually take place at the agency, but occasionally agency scouts are sent to meet prospective clients in their home cities.

An agent who does not request a meeting may wish to see more pho-

rounds of the agencies. Don't be afraid to reapply to the same agency every six months or so. An agency may send a letter of rejection because they currently represent a model with a look similar to yours. Agency rosters are always changing, and there may be a place for you in six months or a year—you never know.

2 THE MODELING AGENCY

Photo: G. Bruckheimer

Your agent will navigate your career, setting in motion a business and promotional plan geared to market fully your unique looks and talent. Your potential will be determined, and your prospects in the various markets anticipated. Whether you are promoted as an editorial model or an advertising print and catalog model, you can have a lucrative and rewarding career.

Most major New York agencies are divided along lines similar to those at Wilhelmina Models. Here, models are managed according to their various strengths and experience—editorial, advertising and catalog, and new model development. Each group has its own set of **bookers.** The bookers are hired by the agency to promote models, coordinate their schedules and negotiate fees. And this is all done from the agency's **boards.** Each division has a board, and this is where all the work and action take place.

Portrait of an Agency

Photo: G. Bruckheimer

The Boards

Wilhelmina's W2

W2 at Wilhelmina, and similar divisions at other agencies, handle the agency's top girls.

Editorial models and models with proven success on the agency's **working board** will move up to the **high board.** These models command the highest fees in the agency and are generally in the most demand. They are the names and faces you recognize on magazine covers, in the editorial pages of fashion magazines, in fragrance and cosmetics ads, in clothing print and television campaigns and on the runways of major designers. Some of these models earn rates topping $15,000 a day!

SELF

Annual Breast
Cancer Report
Update

STRONG,
SEXY &
STRESS-FREE
3 high-speed workouts

Skill for Success:
making a good
first impression

SUPER
SOY
the newest low-cal
wonder food

DIET PILLS
the pros and cons

staying fit
& self-esteem

exercising your
way to a better
self-image

BODY FAT
new ways to measure it

4 SKIN PROBLEMS SOLVED
WHEN DOES YOUR RELATIONSHIP NEED THERAPY?

Self magazine (October 1995)

Photo: Doug Ordway/AMICA

In questa pagina, abito
stretch leggermente
svasato, con scollatura a
cuore, e canotta in
rete di jais, tutto Ritmo di
Perla. (Scarpe Mario
Valentino; calze Franco
Bombana). Nell'altra
pagina, miniabito in
chiffon di Ritmo di Perla.
(Occhiali Ray-Ban;
scarpe Mab Studio; calze
Malerba con lycra).

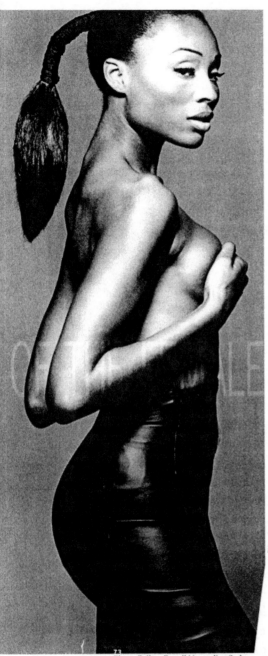

Photo: Bolling Powell/*Australian Style*

The Working Board

Commercial models who work steadily are handled on this board. These models are booked on catalog, advertising, television assignments and on the occasional editorial assignment. Their rates range from $1500 per day to $5000 per day, with additional fees negotiated for advertising bonuses.

December 1995

New Woman

Stress-Free Holiday Enterta

Sex
The Fast
And
Fun Way

Massage
Is It Better
To Give Than
To Receive?

**How To Cope
With Bosses
From Hell**

5 Essential Keys
To Happiness

9 Wa
To Ge
A Gri
On
Ange

5 Wome
Who Se
The Mal
Trends

"Loving A
Autis
Child"

Family
Nudity-
Dos Ar
Don'ts

Astrology Gift Guide

Photo: Jacques Malignon/*New Women* magazine

The Sophisticated Woman Board

In a market where baby boomers represent a large segment of the buying power, the demand for older models is growing. Most of the models on the **sophisticated woman board** are experienced, established professionals who have grown up with the agency and are now in their late twenties, early thirties. The bulk of their bookings involve catalogs and advertising featuring "young moms" promoting household, skin care and health care products.

The Test Board: New Faces

The **test board** of the agency is where new models discover if the business is for them and the agency explores ways of marketing these promising beginners. About 30 percent of the models taken on by a major agency graduate from the test board to the various working boards. The beginning model is sent on go-sees, and the responses of clients, photographers and other industry professionals are carefully monitored. It is hoped that the new model will be tested by photographers, build a portfolio and, with the agency's guidance, develop a strong look on which to base a career. Agents on the test board are constantly reviewing film on their girls, choosing photographs for the

Glamorous fashions for mothers

ALL THAT SHIMMERS

models' portfolios and eventually for composites. They also help models find suitable living arrangements, part-time jobs, if necessary, and advise them on everything from hair, makeup, wardrobe and exercise to dealing with homesickness.

Many new models will be sent to Europe to continue to build their portfolios, to work with influential foreign photographers and to earn the tear sheets (editorial work published in fashion magazines) that will allow them to stand out as accomplished professionals in the competitive New York market.

The 10/20: Plus Size Board

Over 60 percent of women in America wear a size 9 or larger. This substantial segment of the population wants to buy from sources with whom they can identify. They want to see clothing on glamorous women of their own size. Plus size models have similar proportions to their size 6–8 counterparts. They are tall (5'8"–5'11"), have long legs, well-proportioned limbs and torsos and attractive faces, and they wear dress sizes ranging from size 10 to 20. Most of the work

Most of the merchandise in this catalog is available in all Dillard's stores. If your selection is not available, we will gladly order it for you from one of our other stores. Or call our toll-free number.

Photo: Barry Harris/Dillard's

these models book is of the catalog variety, but advertising jobs are sometimes arranged.

Who's Who in the Agency

While most of your communication will be with your agent, it is helpful to know how an agency functions and who does what. The director of the agency oversees the entire operation, talks to the press and determines the agency's direction—what kind of models it will take on and how they will be marketed. The director's job is also a social one. She (or he) will attend the many functions, business and social, that are necessary to build the agency's image and status in the industry. She will appear on talk shows, do interviews and give lectures to promote the agency and will do everything possible to build the agency's reputation and find new and exciting ways to promote the talent it represents. The director is also responsible for choosing the agency staff, the financial people as well as the bookers who will interact directly with the models.

Then there are the division directors. Usually there is a director for the Women's Division and another for the Men's Division. Judy Linton, director of the Women's Division at Wilhelmina Models, describes her responsibilities: "My job is to guide everyone—get them aggressively out there to reach out to all our clients and promote our models. I feel that to do my job well I have to be hands on with the clients, negotiating, interacting with the bookers and the models."

Next, we have the agents (bookers). There will be many or few, depending upon the size of the agency. Agents maintain constant communication with models, photographers and clients. They review the portfolios of photographers who want to interview models for assignments or for test sessions. They organize model portfolios, track down tear sheets, schedule models' appointments and bookings. They talk to the foreign agents who are managing their models who are working abroad. They arrange for transportation, from airline tickets to car services. Finally, they quell disputes between models and clients and make excuses for models arriving late for

the renegotiation of model contracts and advertising bonuses. Secretaries assist in communications within the agency and handle telephone calls from outside. The publicity department, or P.R. agency, prepares agency press releases and promotes and protects the images of the models the agency represents. An army of messengers shuttles model portfolios, agency books and packs of composites back and forth between the agency and its clients. Mailroom workers handle overnight deliveries of portfolios and composite cards, along with the surge of regular mail that goes in and out of an agency daily.

The Model-Agent Relationship

a booking. Because agents deal so directly with the models they represent, we will talk about them at greater length later in the chapter.

A great many other people are involved in the day-to-day workings of an agency. The accounting department handles client billing for all the models and is responsible for issuing checks to the models and the agency staff on a (usually) biweekly basis. They also handle

The model-agent (booker) relationship is a vital one: Some models adopt their bookers as both friends and surrogate parents. Some are satisfied with a purely professional relationship. At the beginning of your career, your agent (or booker) will be your link with your agency and with the entire industry. Well aware of the importance of this relationship, we try to hire agents who are not only professionally well connected but who can empathize with the models they represent. "A good agent," notes Kevin Jones, "understands that modeling is not an easy business, because a model has to face the word 'no' more often in a year than most people will in a lifetime. You're being rejected because you are not the right height or your hair isn't the right color, your nose is a little too broad. You're almost like a target, a human target. A lot of people can't deal with that emotionally."

At the same time, it is important to understand that a booker is responsible for many models—not just you. Be friendly, but try to be professional too. If a close personal relationship develops naturally, that's wonderful, but it's not necessary for your success in the business. Conscientious agents will promote their models equally—taking interest and pride in the accomplishments of every one of them.

Occasionally, a booker may show favoritism. If ever you feel that this is the case at your agency, have a talk with your booker. She (or he) may not be aware of what she is doing. Or there may be a bit of paranoia involved on your part. If you determine that you really are being treated unfairly, and are not being promoted as you should, you may want to consider changing agencies.

Your booker is responsible for promoting you as a model, making sure that you are seen and assessed by the appropriate industry professionals, including photographers, casting agents, art directors, designers and the editors at the fashion magazines. Agents are experts at preparing portfolios and then presenting and promoting a young model to the appropriate clients at the right time.

Bookers are also charged with keeping accurate records and appointments, scheduling a model's time, and meticulously relaying

Photo: C. Bruckheimer

bookings and the particulars of each booking to the model. Your booker will negotiate your fee for each assignment, and the agency will handle all billing and collection. The agent also acts as a buffer between the model and the client. If a dispute should arise, the agent will act as mediator, defending the model against any unfair complaints a client might make.

The ideal model-booker relationship is one of trust, enthusiasm and mutual respect. If these elements are present and both you and your booker are willing to work hard, your career will be on the right track. Kevin Jones describes the constant feedback in a working model-agent relationship: "There's a certain zest that a booker has for a model, pushing them, calling them all the time, helping them build a book, not just taking phone calls. It's very important for a model's success—understanding that. We have to do this together: Who have you seen? How did they respond? How did they treat you in the studio today? Was the hair and makeup good? Let's see the Polaroids. There's a real direct personal contact involved. The career is plotted every day, not only go-sees and bookings, but the model's social life as well. Events must be selected carefully."

The Importance of Good Representation

If you do a little investigating, you'll find that the top models are signed to New York's top five or six agencies. This is no accident. These agencies are expert at scouting and promoting talent. Furthermore, if a model with a less influential agency begins to get a lot of attention, she will usually be snapped up by one of the top agencies. They will offer her the best in representation, career planning and promotion—a package the intelligent model on her way to the top cannot refuse.

The quality of a model's representation can mean the difference between a so-so career and superstardom. So if you are in the fortunate position of being accepted by several agencies, do your homework and choose the one that will best promote you.

Here's one model's account of her less than ideal introduction to the business:

My boyfriend, a photography student, entered a photograph of me in a contest sponsored by a Minneapolis department store and a major jeans manufacturer. I ended up winning the contest, and the prize was a three-day (two-night) all-expenses-paid trip to New York City to meet with agents at two modeling agencies! Was I excited! Well, that's when the trouble started. I was seventeen and had never entertained the thought of becoming a model. I was tall and skinny, gawky and gangly—certainly *not* one of those graceful creatures that swayed confidently through the fashion magazines. I didn't bother to do any research into the industry before my trip. In fact, I thought it pretty funny that the judges had chosen me at all—were they all myopic? I didn't know the names of the reputable agencies in New York, or anything else about modeling. I trusted that the people running the contest wouldn't send me into a minefield.

Because of my school schedule, I opted to go to New York on a Friday (when I had no classes), and stay the weekend.

What I didn't understand at that time of teenage uncertainty was that physically and mentally (if not emotionally), I had everything necessary to do very well as a model. I was seventeen years old, 5'9½", weighed about 118, with a long neck, long slim legs, perfect skin, classic even features, straight shiny long dark hair, and big hazel eyes that until the year before had been hidden behind nerdy, stop-sign-shaped Coke-bottle glasses. I had been a lifeguard and swimming instructor for the past two years and had been swimming a mile a day for at least three years before that, so I was in pretty remarkable physical shape. Furthermore, I had always been a serious and conscientious student with a high grade point average and was more than prepared to transfer that attitude of dedication into the pursuit of a career. What I didn't have was confidence, a knowledge of the industry and expert guidance.

I arrived at New York's La Guardia Airport late Friday morning, caught myself a taxi from the airport to the Milford Plaza Hotel, where a room had been booked for me. My first stroll on the streets of New York City took me straight across town on Forty-second Street. The whistles and catcalls from the wild men of New York didn't bother me as I was pretty sure they were aimed at someone else.

I arrived punctually at my first "agency appointment," on East Fortieth Street, climbed up to the fourth floor and was greeted by the agency's owner, an elderly man (I'll call him Mr. F.) who was limping around, doubled over, complaining about back problems and how it'd been such a busy week at the agency, trying to please *Elle* and *Vogue,* who both insisted on booking the same model at the same time; how he was so exhausted—oh, how his back ached—he'd run out of his medication, had to get home to rest and take his medicine, he was in such pain . . . I was to come with him back to his apartment. Once he took his medication he would feel better. He'd make me a salad and tell me all about the business. New York could be a dangerous place for a young girl, but, he assured me, he would be my "father-figure" while I was here, "tell me all I needed to know, guide me and protect me."

My heart went out to the poor old thing immediately and I half-carried him down to a taxi on Madison Avenue. When we arrived at his apartment building on Seventy-

second Street, he was half-dead with the pain.

Once upstairs (he recovered immediately upon taking his medication), Mr. F. tossed up a big green salad, which he insisted was all I should ever eat from this day forward if I wanted to maintain "that figure." He asked me about myself. How much did I make as a lifeguard? Then he told me that, with his expert guidance, I had huge potential as a model. I could make thousands of dollars a day and be on the covers of the biggest fashion magazines. He then began a long diatribe, describing the dangers of the business and life in New York City: the greedy, sleazy, lying men, the drugs and kidnappings—at the end of which I was quite shaken. But Mr. F. was tired after his speech, and his pain had returned. He decided to retire to his bed, lie in front of the television for a little while to regain his strength. I helped him hobble to his bed. He lay flat on his stomach and asked me to rub his back for a moment. The poor man was in such pain, but I didn't feel at all comfortable with this. Then he rolled over onto his back. Would I rub his legs a little? "U-u-h . . . um," I stuttered. This was too much. "I'd better go now. I, um—promised to call my parents at [I looked at the clock—7:15], um, 7:30. . . ." I babbled.

"Call from here, the phone is—"
he called after me as I ran out the
door . . .

The next morning found me on
East Fifty-ninth Street, on the
doorstep of Ford Models Inc. I rang
the bell. There was no response. It
was Saturday. The agency was
closed. I decided to go for a walk in
Central Park. So much for my first
"interview."

—Jennie C.

Jennie moved to New York
shortly after the episode
she recounts, studied hard
with acting teachers and,
in the next five years, had some
success as an
actress. Finan-
cially, though, she
was not as secure
as she would
have liked.
    Time and
time again,
agents and pho-
tographers approached her, gave
her their cards and asked her to
call. Distrustful, and determined to
be an actress, not a model, she
ignored them. Finally, a friend
dragged her in to an open call at
one of New York's major modeling
agencies. She was astonished by the
professionalism of the agents who
spoke with her, and after a short

trial period on the agency's test
board, she signed with them. When
she was twenty-two, Jennie began
working in Europe and New York,
building an editorial portfolio and
earning a very good income. She
hopes one day to be able to channel
her success as a model into a career
as an actress.
    Jennie's advice to beginning
models:

Modeling is a youth-driven industry. You don't have much time
to make mistakes. So know what
you want, know where you fit in the
industry, do your research, get good
representation, and once you are on
your way, maintain an attitude of
professionalism.

Choosing an Agency

Let's say you are lucky
enough to be accepted by
more than one agency.
How do you decide which
one to work with? Ask yourself the
following questions: Is the agent
professional and enthusiastic about
working with you? Does the agent
seem to believe in you and in your
potential for success? Where is the

agency's place in the competition? What caliber of models does it represent? Successful models? Supermodels? Factor all these things into your choice. Above all, when choosing amongst equally good agencies, the chemistry you have with its people should be the deciding factor. After all, this business is largely about human relationships. Sign with the agency you feel most comfortable with.

3 THE BEGINNING MODEL

What does the agency expect from you, its model client? Agencies expect dedication and professionalism. The industry is so competitive that an unreliable or unprofessional model will be replaced almost instantly by someone of similar looks and talent, but with a better attitude—scary, eh?

Bear in mind that confirmed bookings are considered sacred in this industry. Once you have agreed to a booking, you are expected to arrive on time and prepared. You may be held responsible for a job's fee if you don't call the agency in time for them to find an appropriate replacement. The success of a photo or commercial shoot is dependent upon an entire crew conscientiously fulfilling their responsibilities. That includes you, the model hired for the shoot. A photo shoot is a highly organized operation, planned well in advance. Budgets can be enormous, and the end result is only as strong as its weakest link. That's why agencies expect models to be organized, professional and willing to do the job to the best of their ability.

At Wilhelmina, we expect our beginning models to observe the following guidelines:

1 Look neat and clean. Hair should be combed and clothing "crisp" looking. Nails should be clean and manicured.

The Model's Responsibility to the Agent

2 Always call in to your agent between 5:00 and 5:30 P.M. daily for your next day's schedule. Don't make us frantic locating you for tomorrow's booking. We lose sleep over stuff like this.

3 Let the agency know as far as possible in advance when you want to book out for vacations, or personal reasons. Scheduling can become very complex when a model is in demand—your agents need all the help they can get.

4 Always give the agency's phone number (not your own) to prospective clients. This makes you appear professional and will dis-

courage unwanted phone callers. Furthermore, most agents have developed a knack for weeding out the weirdos that models invariably attract.

5 Arrive on time for bookings. If it's unavoidable that you are going to be late, call the agency so that they can ring ahead and cover for you. Agents are very good at this. When you do arrive at your booking, the client will simply be thankful to have you—rather than angry, worried sick that the shoot is ruined and ready to blame anything that might go wrong on you.

Judy Linton summarizes the responsibilities of the model on assignment: "A model must *deliver*. If you are being paid $1500+ for a day's work, the photographer would like you to be attentive. He wants you to move this way—just do it. I've had situations when a photographer has called up and said, 'It's not going to happen. She's pretty, but it's not going to happen. Send me another model. I don't care which other model, just send me another one.' So, you see, there's more to it than just being a beautiful face."

Getting Organized

Once you have an agency, you'll need to invest in a few items to organize your business. Since your agency must be able to reach you at a moment's notice for last-minute go-sees, and bookings, an answering machine is essential, and you must maintain constant contact with it, calling in every hour to retrieve your messages.

You will also need to organize

Thursday NOVEMBER 2
1995 — Day 306 — 59 days to come

APPOINTMENTS — MEMORANDA

8:00
8:30 YM MAGAZINE   CONT: SARA GAYNOR
9:00   685 THIRD AVENUE
9:30   4TH FLOOR
10:00 SEVENTEEN MAGAZINE CONT: DONNA
10:30   850 THIRD AVENUE
11:00 FRANUS LONG STUDIO 112 W. 31St. ST.
11:30   (BRING BATHING SUIT)
12:00 AGENCY - TO SEE PHOTOGRAPHER - DOUG
12:30 ORDWAY RE: VERSACE #786-9863
1:00
1:30
2:00 PETER LERY - HAIR PRODUCTS
2:30   119 W. 22nd ST
3:00 KEVIN KNER + ASSOCIATES
3:30 CASTING FOR SHOW WEEK - VARIOUS
4:00   84 WOOSTER ST
4:30   CONT: TOM HOPKINS
5:00   RE: TESTING
5:30 PICK UP MORE COMP CARDS AT AGENCY!
6:00 JOHN BELL - PICKUP
CONTACT SHEETS

7:00 CHECK WILHELMINA.
COM FOR EMAIL!

EXPENSE RECORD
BREAKFAST   ENTERTAINMENT
LUNCH 5   AUTO
DINNER   MISC MANICURE
HOTEL   12
TIPS
FARES TAXI 8.50
POSTAGE   SUBWAY 3.00
PHONE CALLS 1.75 TOTAL

your schedule with an efficient day planner. One day to a page is the best layout to record go-sees, bookings, travel information and expenses. Make copies of your entries from time to time and file them in a safe place. If your book is lost, you will still have a record of your itemizations for tax purposes. Trying to reconstruct these at tax time can be a nightmare—one that is easily prevented by taking this simple precaution.

ues to book work, her portfolio will grow, change and improve. A successful model's book is always changing—current tear sheets replacing those of the year before.

Once a portfolio is underway, it is important that several copies be

The Portfolio

Perhaps your most important promotional tool as a model is a portfolio of photographs that show you at your best. Frequently a client will see your book before they see you. They may browse through hundreds of model portfolios from several different agencies before choosing which models they would like to see in person. For this reason it is important that you build the strongest portfolio you can. It will take the determined beginner a year to build a book that is competitive in the New York market. During that year the agency will arrange for you to test with photographers. You will also be expected to travel to various foreign markets to book the editorial assignments that will help you create a strong look and an impressive, professional portfolio. As a model contin-

prepared and kept up to date. One will accompany the model on all go-sees and assignments. Several will be kept at the agency, ready to be sent out to clients at their request. Additional copies will be kept on hand by a model's foreign agents so that they may be shown to local clients and photographers.

Agents arrange a model's portfolio with care and a trained eye. They want to create the greatest possible impact on the client viewing the book. You may not always agree with their decisions. If you find that a favorite photograph is removed from your portfolio, it's probably for the best. Agents know their clients and are well aware of the ever-changing trends in the industry. So have that special photo framed and hang it on the wall of your apartment where *you* can enjoy it!

The Composite

O nce you have some exceptional photographs in your portfolio, your agent will put together a composite. The composite is a valuable promotional tool, because it will be sent to important prospective clients in order to secure work for the model. The cost of printing composites varies according to the requirements of the agency. If a model is new, her first composite may be a simple color Xerox of a flattering test shot, accompanied by the model's name and statistics. Other composites consist of a single photograph. Some are two-sided with four or more photos. Still others open out like greeting cards and are mini-portfolios in themselves. One New York agency even sends out printed booklets on its models! Most agencies have composite racks, which provide a slot for each model's composite card.

Photo: G. Bruckheimer

A gencies use various promotional tools to enhance the reputation of the agency and the models it represents. The model book and head sheet sent out to clients reflect the agency's status in the industry. Thus, the quality of these publications is of prime importance. Sometimes small agencies will try to impress with gimmicks. I

The Agency Book and Head Sheet

have seen model agency books that are laid out as editorial magazines; books where a particular model's name and statistics have been printed next to the back of her head, but she is nowhere else to be seen in the book! Other gimmicks include mailing books of photographs printed on handmade paper, nestled in a box with wrapping paper and wild flowers. This may be a lovely sentiment, but how will it hold up to photographers, stylists, clients, makeup- and hairstylists, reps, and casting agents if, in their constant model searches, they must refer to this book every day for six months? I find that the best agency books are sturdy volumes with

fingerprint-resistant paper stock and clear strong photographs (shot by the better-known photographers) of the models represented. These books are expensive to produce, and you will be expected to pay a portion of the cost. After all, it's you who's being promoted. With your approval, anywhere from $200 to $1500 (depending on your agency and the type of book) will be deducted from your future earnings.

The agency head sheet is an excellent tool because it is designed so that clients will hang it on their office wall for easy reference. The head sheet is poster sized, with the name and a beauty shot of each of the models represented by the agency.

Photo: G. Bruckheimer

Electronic Promotion

The speed and efficiency of the computer world is having a huge impact on business, and the modeling industry is no exception. Casting agents, art directors—well, anyone who frequently hires models—can subscribe to programs that pull up photographs and statistics at the touch of a key. Say a client needs a 5'10" size 6–8 blue-eyed brunette for an upcoming project. He inputs these variables, and within seconds, photographs of all the models in the data base who match this description are made available to him on-screen. Agencies are also using the Internet as a promotional tool. Want to know the latest industry gossip, or see photographs of up-and-coming model superstars? Just log on! All this is great for the modeling industry. It creates excitement and makes the business of "selling" images all the more lively, entertaining and accessible.

THE **W**ILHELMINA WEB

CLICK HERE TO REGISTER FOR FREE INFO

Photo of Michael Bergin by Michael Tammaro. Photo of Michelle Weweje by Nadir

W FEMALE MODELS

W $100,000 MODEL SEARCH

W SITE INFO

W MODEL NEWS WIRE

W MODEL MERCHANDISE

W MALE MODELS

Check out our top male and female models, learn behind the scenes news, get tips from the pros, enter a model search or order some official Wilhelmina Model merchandise. If this is your first time, don't forget to register today - it's FREE and the first 100 are eligible to win an official Wilhelmina Internet Cap.

MODEL

http://www.wilhelmina.com

A Day in the Life of the Model

Your day actually begins the night before, with a call to your agency between 5:00 and 5:30 P.M. every weekday for the following day's schedule. At this time, your booker will give you the day's booking(s), go-sees or auditions. Write these down carefully in your day planner, double-checking all times and addresses. Much of your time as a young model will be spent on the go, presenting yourself and your portfolio to photographers and prospective clients. In a large city such as New York, a number of young models represented by the same agency may share an apartment in order to keep expenses down and to have roommates (and, hopefully, friends) in the same business, with whom they can identify. Models often attend go-sees together, exercise together and share the excitement, rewards and disappointments of the business.

Most go-sees, bookings and auditions are scheduled from 8:00 A.M. to 5:30 P.M. weekdays. Depending upon their exercise schedules (morning or evening), most models are up between 6:30 and 7:30 A.M. A model should arrive at a booking with clean hair and face. A little makeup can be applied for go-sees, but this is usually limited to lip gloss and mascara. Hair must be neat and away from the face. Studio bookings can last anywhere from one hour (for a fitting or a single shot for a catalog) to eight hours. Overtime is always a possibility, and it may mean extra payment at one and a half times your fee.

Sessions on location may mean travel time and can last anywhere from a single day to weeks. In the case of *trips*, bookings for editorial stories, advertising or catalogs that require extended periods away from home, the client will pay all expenses for travel, meals and hotel.

A Day in the Life of a Model

Photo: G. Bruckheimer

7:30 A.M.—Rising early to start the day. Notice the crowded apartment, which is very unlike *Models Inc.,* but typical.

7:45 A.M.—Keeping your teeth clean and bright is a very important factor. Remember, your smile is one of your best assets.

8:30 A.M.—Flagging down a cab en route to a *YM* shoot at Industria. I have left myself plenty of time so I won't be late. Clients hate lateness.

10:45 A.M.—Modeling involves a lot of waiting, so I catch up on a personal toenail painting.

12:00 P.M.—Lunch. Notice the bagels, water and orange juice. All have very little or no fat content.

Photo: G. Bruckheimer

Photo: G. Bruckheimer

Photo: G. Bruckheimer

Photo: G. Bruckheimer

Photo: G. Bruckheimer

Photo: G. Bruckheimer

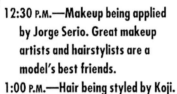

12:30 P.M.—Makeup being applied by Jorge Serio. Great makeup artists and hairstylists are a model's best friends.

1:00 P.M.—Hair being styled by Koji.

2:00–2:29 P.M.—On the telephone, checking in with agency and friends. Since I don't have a set schedule or office, the telephone is my link to the world.

2:30 P.M.—On the set with last-minute hair touch-up.

5:15 P.M.—Meeting at Wilhelmina offices with my booker, David Grilli—receiving tomorrow's schedule.

6:30 P.M.—When I work out, no one knows I'm a model, and I relax to my CD player—essential for the constant traveling.

Runway models do a circuit of shows twice a year, participating in the collections in Paris, Milan and New York. Top runway girls are usually successful print models as well. They may do as many as five or six shows in a single day and make as much as $15,000 per show! This is an exhausting schedule, but it only happens twice a year. For many models, the earnings and exposure are worth the aching feet.

THE
4 WORK

Every model hopes to be featured in the fashion pages and on the cover of *Vogue, Harper's Bazaar* or *Elle.* A model booked for one of these prestigious covers will earn just $100 to $400 for the session, and the editorial pages of the top fashion magazines pay comparably. But once a model appears on such a cover, her career enters high gear—she will be booked for the major fashion advertising campaigns, appear on the catwalks of renowned designers and be counted among the top models considered for lucrative contract work—for fragrance, cosmetics and fashion campaigns. Carefully managed by her agent, she will be in a position to earn millions of dollars a year. That's why editorial work is so sought after by young models working on their portfolios. It is for those editorial tear sheets that models make the rounds of photographers and magazines in cities as diverse as Milan, Italy, and Sydney, Australia.

But all editorial is not created equal. For example, a model may be booked for an "editorial" assignment to illustrate an editorial (non-advertising) story in a fashion magazine. When she picks up the magazine at the newsstand, she may be disappointed to find that

the photograph that took all day to "get just right" has been reproduced the size of a postage stamp beside a short article commenting on current hair color trends. This photograph is useless in a model's

Editorial Print

portfolio. An agent may promote a model for this type of work if she (or he) feels it will get the model noticed by a magazine's editorial staff. Hopefully, the next editorial assignment will be in the magazine's fashion pages illustrating the season's collections and photographed by an established photographer. These full-page fashion editorial photos are the ones that build a portfolio.

The editorial model will avoid using standard (catalog) poses during an editorial shoot unless specifically instructed to do so. A creative ease of movement and a sense of improvisation are the qualities the editorial model must develop. The photographer and photo editor are looking for that one shot (out of several rolls of film) that will catch the attention of the viewer. They will often choose an unusual or "off" photograph—one that is particularly free, natural or unique looking. Editorial work requires a real mixing of talents on the part of

Photo: Eika Aoshima

Photo: Eika Aoshima

style

the crew involved. Everyone—fashion editor, photographer, hair and makeup artists and models—must work together to create the mood of the photograph. A model who is capable of responding instinctively to the vision of the photographer or art director and who can take direction well will excel at editorial print. "Sometimes the sensibility for editorial is innate," adds agent Kevin Jones, "but I think it can be learned as part of the process of understanding style and understanding fashion. It's a lot of dreaming. A model who has seen a lot of movies will know what to do when a photographer walks in and says, 'Be Audrey Hepburn.' If a model has not seen an Audrey Hepburn film, she has no idea who this person is. So there's that training, the knowledge of the past, of fashion and style and a genuine interest in it. You are only as versatile as your education and what you've been exposed to [allow you to be]. The model who tends to become an interesting editorial star is one who has been exposed to a lot of things. The more the model is exposed to something, the greater the range of motion and expression she has to pull from, whereas someone who doesn't have that background tends to be limited. It's an attitude that makes the editorial model shine. An attitude, a sense of personal style, a zest for fashion."

il nero recita a
SOGGETTO

**Tra le improbabili dune
di un deserto metropolitano,
sullo sfondo di una spiaggia
caraibica a Manhattan o
sospesi su un cielo pieno di
nuvole, vanno in scena
ricami, chiffon e paillettes
per una sera glamour**

Nella Favelli - Foto Doug Ordway
Testi Bettina Jacomini
Ha collaborato Leda Gargano

Photo: Doug Ordway/AM/CA

On an editorial booking, points out Judy Linton, "depending on the magazine, the photographer, the type of fashion story, anything can happen and can be incorporated into the creative process. The model can be skinny, voluptuous, ugly, beautiful, ethnic or unusual looking—whatever fits the story. Anything goes!"

Catalog

Catalog is the bread and butter of the typical working model. Models are hired by companies who want to sell their clothing to the public through brochures and mail-order catalogs. They need attrac-tive people to make those clothes look appealing. Catalog bookings can range from one-hour engage-ments to shoot a single garment to week-long assignments on location. Rates range from $150 per hour or $1200 to $2500 per day, so a model

who books a lot of catalog work can make a very good annual income.

The main concern of the model booked on a catalog job is to show off the clothing. Great care will be taken by the crew to light the clothing properly, see that it fits well and is wrinkle free. Less attention is paid to the model, her lighting and appearance. Usually, a model is lit satisfactorily and her makeup applied carefully, with a light hand, but it is wise to know how to touch up your own makeup, which angles are your best in front of the camera and which angles show off the clothing to the greatest advantage.

Unlike an editorial shoot, where two to five shots may be executed in a day, as many as fourteen shots may be completed in the course of a day's catalog shoot. The efficient, professional model, who gets the job done with a minimum of fuss, will be hired over and over again for this type of work. Judy Linton, director of the Women's Division at Wilhelmina, explains that "A catalog model is more of an everyday type of girl, the girl-next-door kind of look. Think of the Chadwick's catalog, and who buys from that catalog. These people want to see someone in the clothes with whom they can identify. They don't want

to see a very skinny model, or anyone too unusual or unique looking."

Advertising

Depending on the particular clothing line and client preferences, fashion shots for advertising can be done in a catalog style or a more editorial style. The purpose of an advertisement is to sell clothing, cosmetics or a fragrance, or to promote a line of clothing along

Photo: Michael Thompson/Coty

with a designer or company name. Rates for advertising work are generally higher than catalog rates and, depending on usage (magazine, point of purchase, billboard, etc.) and length of usage, bonuses can sometimes be earned on top of the daily rate.

Exclusive or "contract" advertising rates are much higher, because the client must pay an exclusivity fee to the model and her agent as compensation for other work that they must turn down.

Runway

There is nothing like the runway experience. Runway models describe the energy of the live audience and the moment of connecting with the photographers on the runway—they are actually calling out to you throughout the show. A model can hear them screaming. You have to know where your *points* are. If you stop midpoint on the runway, the photographers will get a beautiful head to toe shot. At the end of the runway, it's a bodice shot, so you must give them a beautiful face. Going back, pause at midpoint, because the back of the dress is beautiful. Turn your head slightly so they get a little bit of profile. Then a nice pause at the top of

Red or dead

Photo: Alex Zoetos/Balagan

the stage, with the designer's name behind your head. A model must know these things. She can take lessons or learn by watching the shows on television.

Runway is more important than ever before. At one time you were either a runway girl or a print girl. Today the overlap is enormous. The runway model is the editorial

Photo: Robert Kirk/Ralph Lauren

model. These are the faces on the magazines. "Runway today," stresses Judy, "is like a big go-see worldwide. The designers see you. The photographers see you. The magazine editors see you." Most successful print models eventually make appearances on the runways of the designers whose print campaigns they've done. Some take to it with confidence, grace and style. Others need a little encouragement to develop finesse on the catwalk. Some models start off on the runway, are spotted by a photographer or designer and are launched into successful careers as print models.

Paris-based runway expert Jay Alexander discusses the lifestyle of the runway model and the art of walking.

Your work centers around the world's catwalks. How did this happen?

Very simple. Monique Pillard, president of Elite [Model Management], encouraged me. She said, "You're really great in shows. You should go to Tokyo," and I flew to Tokyo thinking, "I'm too tall and I'm too ugly . . .

Why am I doing this?" But Monique told me, "No, you have a great sense of style. You move incredibly on the catwalk, you should go." And it went in one ear and came out the other.

So you didn't go?

Finally I *did* go to Tokyo—quite an interesting experience for me. Then I came back, and several new young designers who had been doing shows in clubs began asking, "Can we use you? You'd be really great in the show." So I was doing those shows in Limelight, Palladium and places like that. Then I was encouraged to go to Paris. I went to Paris, and they were interested in me only because I was the male model who had female pictures of himself in his book. The first half of my book was all male. The second half was all female. It was kind of interesting for that time. People would call me in on castings to see if I was real or some freak of nature. Today, of course, it would be no big deal. But, after a while, it wasn't happening for me in Paris, so I said, "[I'd better] take my black ass back to America where I live."

I'm from the South Bronx, and one out of nine children. I'm number six. Born April 12, 19—I don't remember. And after that I went back to New York, and Betina Reims—a very good photographer—booked me for a book she was doing on androgyny. And she said, "Stay, stay longer, people just aren't used to you yet." I say, "Yeah, but I can't afford to stay here. I'm starving." I mean, I was buying croissants without the butter because they are cheaper. "Hello," I'm saying to myself. "Well, I can always go back home and eat."

How did you get into the business of teaching runway to the world's aspiring models?

The whole thing of teaching the models how to walk just kind of happened. I was just hanging out and watching the shows, and had nothing to do. You weren't doing them, so you watched. It's like those who can't—teach. You know what I mean.

Your talent on the runway: Is it just natural—a born talent—or did you develop it?

It could be a combination. Being 6'3½", you don't want to walk hunched over, because it's an awful look and plus it hurts your back. Walking on a runway in high heels you can hurt your back too, but it's only something you do temporarily. But I think for me this whole thing came from—I used to use the words "making fun of," but I think a couple of girls got insulted when I said it on TV. I didn't mean it to hurt anyone's feelings, it was just that I *was* basically imitating models—the way they walk down the runway. I just imitate, you know, I can imitate expressions and things like that—just what I feel that they look like, because I'm really not in front of a mirror doing it. And when I do see myself in front of the mirror doing it, I sort of like laugh. Because it's like a fashion illustration, you overexaggerate. Everyone asks me to do it—just name a girl—immediately I can go into it. You go right down to the voice, and you go into how they whine and how they complain. It's part of everything, and that just came from watching the shows. "Oh, my God, did you see her? She was so fabulous! She was walking

Photo: Michel Nafziger

like this." And I would imitate the walk. I would just imitate the walk. But, as I said, I try to be careful, because we're in a very sensitive business. The majority of the girls that I see come in all have something different or special about them. They just need to go with it.

Is that what you try to encourage in the model when you are teaching?
Yeah, that's very important. You build that confidence—like I would say, "Keep your happy-sponsor smile." It is kind of like, you know, a girl comes in, posture is off, looks bad. Walk, any girl can walk.

That's what I've heard, that you can teach anybody to walk. Now is that really true, or does it take a certain amount of innate talent?
It takes a bit of talent—first of all, honey, in order to *do my job*. If it's all about walking—anybody can walk. If you actually put those high heels on and have that makeup on and walk down someone's runway, no matter how big the designer or how small, you have done it. You have had the experience. You see the shows. You know what they want. Some designers don't change from season to season as far as what they like done on the runway. My job is to help a girl with those techniques, with the art of walking—what to do in the clothing to make herself stand out, look confident. What's special

about her, should work for her. Her job as a model is to be able to adapt to Comme des Garçons at twelve o'clock in the afternoon, after having just come from doing Karl Lagerfeld at ten—with different makeup, different attitude, different music, a different way of moving. For Comme des Garçons, she has just cut all the hip movement, all the arm swinging—just be very straight and no-nonsense down the runway. She must be able to run from there and be very intense and very strong for Christian Dior. Then go be full of personality and drama for Mugler. After that, fun and flippant for Gaultier. These are things that are very important. Also, what girls don't realize, you go up for a show, you walk into the room, honey, they've *already seen you walking!* They may ask you to walk—I mean, you turn and you walk away from them to go to the spot where you're told to start your walk *from*—it's too late. You get, "We'll see, thank you very much." That's a big no-no. Also, girls go in thinking they're supposed to have personality. They talk too damn much, blah, blah, blah . . .

What are the qualifications of the runway model?
Confidence, good legs, I don't think you have to be pretty to go down the runway. You have to be able to carry a garment, to make a garment come alive. If I was a designer, I wouldn't

really want to see a girl's book. That wouldn't interest me. I would just ask the girl to walk. And if I liked how she looked, and if I really wanted to use her, I would then say to her, "Okay, work on this. Work on that." I'd give her maybe two or three outfits that are being used in the show, just to feel it out. And then let her actually have that experience onstage. Some designers do that. Some designers tell the girls, "I want you to walk like this." Now I don't want everybody using this approach all of a sudden just because I'm media-popular! Other people have been doing this for years [teaching runway], but it just so happens that I am the one that is being chased down by the press.

Why are you getting so much attention?

Well, a number of models who have been my friends—who I helped when they were starting out—have become very successful.

Let's have some names.

Claudia Mason, Susan Holmes, Nadja Auermann, Heather Stuart-Whyte, Patricia Hartmann. These are girls who have been my friends, girls that I have advised and given a few lessons—two or three. It's not that I am trying to make every girl perfect, no one is perfect. It's just to give them that confidence. Meghan Douglas is another one. And working with her was like pulling teeth, because it was like "Do you really want it?" Finally, after the fifth time it was kind of like—well, we had a long discussion. I see her now—I grin from ear to ear. I see her really putting it to work. And she's really changed her way of thinking—from combat boots and flannel shirts to pumps and dresses. For me it is something: if I see the girl go down the runway, and she is quite comfortable with it, then my job is done.

What if a model is really scared, really nervous on the runway, what do you say?

Usually I ask a girl when she comes in the door, "Are you interested in doing shows?" If the girl says to me, "No, my agent wants me to do it, but I really don't want to," I get on the phone, call up the agency and say, "This girl is useless." But if she says, "Yes, I want to do shows. I have to do shows, but I'm scared to death," I say, "Okay, fine." And, I'll ask, "What is it that you are scared about?" If she says to me, "Being in front of people," then she's in the wrong business. If she says, "I know I'll love it if I can be confident, but I get shaky up there," then let's start. And don't be afraid to make mistakes. You are allowed to make mistakes. That is very important. You're not going to go out there and do everything perfectly. If I make a mistake, you don't see it because I won't make a face. I just keep on going. There are girls who say they don't like doing shows but have to do them in order to be abreast of what's going on and to be seen. Okay, so keep it simple. Anybody can walk. You walk here, you walk to school, whatever. You can walk. It's just that now we make it look good, turn it into an art form.

What about those high heels?

That's another thing too. All of a sudden some big famous photographer comes into the countryside to use it for a location and sees this girl milking a cow and taking the cheese into the shed, and it's kind of like, "Oh, my God, you're so beautiful. Have you ever thought about modeling?" And the girl never realized how beautiful she was, because she's been in a town of three people. Her, her mother and her father. Of course your mother isn't going to tell you if you are the ugliest sow in the world, it's "Look at my beautiful baby. Look at my beautiful child." So you are taken from there, you're put into the fashion world. Then you have to grow up. You are 14, 15 years old. Now you have to grow up. *Fast.* You have to start wearing high heels. You never wore high heels before. And your first couture gown was your christening dress. Now you're thrown down into a chair—somebody puts makeup on you, false eyelashes, lots of powder,

you feel you look ugly, because you aren't comfortable with it. It's something you are not used to. Once you become used to it, then you start buying the magazines to see what everybody else is looking like. Then you start listening to other models talking on interviews or see them on TV. You begin to emulate or imitate, "This is what I am supposed to be doing. Where do I fit in?" You become nervous because you feel that you must make the people at Christian Dior happy because they're hiring you. You want to show them you can do a great job. *And the pressure is on.* I had one girl the other day who said, "I went to Dior. They asked me to walk, and I blew it. They told me to come back when I can walk." I said, "That's because they like you." Usually you don't get that chance to go back and see anybody. They don't have time. There are thousands of girls to choose from. And you have to go through the whole process of waiting on line for casting, stockings, shoes too small, or shoes too big. Getting dressed—like ten pounds on your back, with all the bustle and the rigmarole and the taffetas and the crinolines and the velvets. And they want you to run down the runway like you are light as a feather. What do you do? The only things you've ever worn are a pair of jeans and a shirt tied around your waist and a pair of boots. Now you're in high heels. It's very, very, hard for some. There are girls who fantasize growing up that they want to be a model, and they'll do whatever it takes to get there. When they ask you at the fitting, you know, "Are your shoes okay?" you are afraid to say they are too big or too small—afraid you are not going to get the job. So what do you do? You suffer. If they say, "Do you like your dress?" and you think it is the most hideous thing in the world, you say "It's beautiful. I love it." . . . God-awful ugly. "I see you putting on that big smile," I say, "Honey, you just have to be ugly for about two minutes. At some shows, if the makeup is horrible, you have to be ugly for at least an hour."

Do models deserve the fees they get for runway appearances?
They do get paid a lot—don't they? But, yes, it's a lot of work. You've started working at six o'clock in the morning for a nine o'clock show. And you are starving yourself because you don't have time to eat. So you are running all day long. You do appear all over the magazines, in runway shot after runway shot, and are not paid for those pictures. Still, to deserve the money, you must not take it for granted. You must put in the effort. We are very fortunate, and I'm very lucky I

look the way I do. I really feel that I am blessed, and everybody else that is doing this job is blessed. Some are more fortunate than others. Some will make more money than others, but I can still walk in my door with my head the same size it was before all this happened.

Jay's Tips for Runway Models
1. Be yourself.
2. Accentuate your most positive features.
3. Don't be afraid to make mistakes.
4. Let other models inspire you, but don't try to walk like them. Develop your own personal signature on the runway.

Television Commercials

Many models make the transition into television commercials smoothly. Film is film, and the moving camera takes to the model's face just as well as the still camera does. That's why models are in great demand for television, film work, music videos and the like. You will broaden your opportunities in this area by becoming proficient at reading copy in front of a camera. It takes some practice to make readings sound natural, so you might want to invest in an on-camera commercial or acting class. These are usually taught by casting directors, who are more than happy to recommend their hand-trained "graduates" for some of the productions they cast. Your agency will be able to recommend a class for you to attend. From time to time, classes are held especially for models breaking into commercials.

There is a great deal of money to be made in television commercials. A television spot that runs nationally can pay tens of thousands of dollars in residuals in the course of its lifetime. Principal performers (those featured in commercials) make money in the form of residuals every time a spot is aired. If you have a number of spots airing at the same time, your income can add up dramatically without any additional days of work on your part. Furthermore, once you are a member of Screen Actors Guild, the union that regulates the film industry on behalf of talent, and you have made a requisite amount of money in the period of a year, you will receive free health care. So you may find it worthwhile, with the help of your agency, to prepare and promote yourself in this lucrative area.

5 OPPORTUNITIES IN SPECIALTY MODELING

No, you don't have to be 5'9" and weigh 115 pounds to be a model. The opportunities are out there: for attractive women who wear a dress size 10 to 20, for aspiring models smaller than size 6/8 or 6–8 and for men and women with especially photogenic hands, feet, legs, lips, torsos—even ears! Here's a breakdown of the avenues open to you as a specialty model.

Plus Size Modeling

Plus size models range in dress size from size 10 to size 20. They must meet many of the same requirements as straight size models—with perfect skin and even features, long legs in proportion to the torso, a long neck and they must be able to move well in front of a camera. Most plus size models are 5'8" to 5'11" tall, bust 36" to 42", waist 26" to 32", hips 36" to 45", and weigh 140 to 170 lbs. More and more catalogs are expanding to include larger sizes, so beautiful proportionate models are more in demand than ever. To meet the growing market, several of New York's top agencies, including Wilhelmina Models and Ford Models, have opened divisions representing larger size "10/20" models. We talked to one agent who books 10/20 models:

What kind of work is available to 10/20 models?
They do catalogs, Spiegel for You Catalog, Appleseed for You, lots of that stuff. They are also doing ads, campaigns for Merit cigarettes, and, when a magazine like *Cosmopolitan* needs a fuller-figured model for a story, they are doing editorial.

What do you look for in a 10/20 model?
First, she has to look like a model. I see girls size 9, and from size 10 through 20. I'll even look at a really full 8. Perhaps she's a little fuller in the hips, or fuller in the face. On my board I have every size, 8 through 20. Within each size I have a blond, a brunette, a redhead and one of each to back them up. Most of all, I look for models who move well in front of the camera.

How does a 10/20 model get started?
Just send me pictures! Snapshots are my favorite thing—one full head shot, one full body. That's it.

Photo: Randall Bachner/*Glamour* magazine

Photo: Fadil Berisha

Fashion Workshop

"Give me a break! I'm no size 10"

Smart, sexy, stylish clothes for full figures

CONSIDER THIS: The average fashion model is 5'9" to 6', weighs 123 pounds and wears a size 8; the average American woman is 5'4", weighs 142 pounds and wears a size 14 to 16. Many of us wear 18 and up. Until recently, few in the fashion business addressed this reality, but with sales in plus sizes accelerating at nearly twice the rate of women's apparel overall, more manufacturers and retailers are stepping up to meet the demands of the market.

We asked a group of plus-size models to try on clothes from a variety of regular and plus-size lines. As they browsed, tried on and traded, they **selected** the greatest flatterers, told us what they **wished** they could find and revealed their **personal style strategies** and secrets. On these four pages, we share their finds—and thoughts—with you.

WISH #1: TO FIND A WELL-CUT PANTSUIT IN A QUALITY FABRIC The soft shaping and fluid fabric of this tailored suit compliment womanly curves. Marina Rinaldi wool/acrylic jacket $450, and pants, $250 (sold as suit). Craig Taylor shirt. Lee Revard earrings. Kenneth Cole boots.

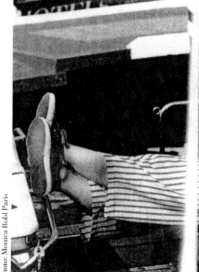

Photo: Monica Robel Paris

How is a 10/20 model promoted?

The same way straight size models are: a model builds a portfolio, a composite card is made, agency books are printed and sent out to prospective clients. Really, the only difference is that our models don't have to go to Europe to build a portfolio. They can do it through testing here in New York.

And what can a 10/20 model expect to earn?

The rates are basically the same as for straight size modeling—$1200 to $1500 day rate for catalog work. Advertising rates are negotiated by the agent. I have models who are earning six-figure salaries yearly. And 10/20 models can also model longer than straight size women. I have a forty-five-year-old woman on my board who works all the time.

Any advice for the beginning model?

Yes, know your body—whatever size you may be. Know how it can move. That's the main thing. I tell all my girls to go study ballet.

Model Pamela Dodson started as a straight size model at the age of nineteen. Maintaining a dress size 8 was difficult, and Pamela found herself battling constantly with her weight. After weathering a distressful period of "weighing in" at her agency every day before being allowed to go on go-sees, she decided to give modeling a break. A year later her agency opened a plus size division. Pamela, a curvy size 10, was now told that she had to *gain weight* before the agency would represent her as a plus size model. That was eight years ago. Pamela now maintains a size 12 and has never been happier with her career. "I really like the market I'm in," she explains. "It's very different from straight size modeling. There is a feeling of friendship and camaraderie in the plus size market that I missed when I modeled straight sizes. I really enjoy the women I work with— there just doesn't seem to be the tension involved. These models are established. There is less turnover. They're a little older. I think that maturity factor makes the working atmosphere more pleasant. And the market is expanding every day. *Glamour* just did a beautiful editorial spread on large sizes in the October issue. I think it's very progressive!"

At one time there were entire agencies devoted to representing petite models. Petite was defined as 5'2" to 5'7", dress size 3–7 Petite. These models had similar proportions to straight size girls—long legs for their height, long necks and measurements 1" to 2" smaller in bust/waist/hip than their straight size counterparts. But

Petite Modeling

these agencies, and consequently the models they represented, didn't seem to thrive.

Today, hopeful petites are mixed in with straight size models and represented by major agencies such as Wilhelmina, Ford and Elite. An exceptionally beautiful girl with scaled down proportions can become very successful, particularly as a beauty model, that is, one whose face is usually featured. Magazine covers, beauty ads, product endorsements, television commercials and, for women who look to be in their teens, juniors (junior sizes 5–7) modeling are all opportunities available to the petite model. While most petite models do not show clothing on the couture runways, there are exceptions. We have already discussed the explosive career of petite (at 5'6") supermodel Kate Moss. Kate has been a featured attraction on the runways of major designers for many seasons. She carries the clothing well and holds her own with the taller models.

Petites eager to get started in modeling should be aware of a few encouraging facts: Most fashion designers have petite lines. Height is not a requirement for beauty modeling. That means you don't have to be 5'9" to appear on the cover of a magazine, in cosmetics campaigns or on the packaging for beauty products. Very tall girls usually do not make successful parts models. Their hands and feet just appear too big on film. The petite model's delicate proportions are often more suitable for this kind of work.

If you want to eventually move toward a career in television or film, being petite may work to your advantage. How many leading men are 6' tall or taller? While there are some successful actresses who are very tall, the majority are between 5'2" and 5'8". So don't listen to the people who've been telling you "You're not tall enough to be a model." Get out there and take advantage of the many opportunities.

You see them everywhere, on the cover of *Vogue*, on product packaging, advertisements and television commercials—**body parts models**. You may not recognize them at first, but if you look at those hands or feet closely, you'll notice that they are familiar. In fact, many of the hands, legs and other body parts attached to various celebrities on magazine covers and product endorsements are not their own, but those of a model chosen for the job precisely because of his/her photogenic body parts.

Most female hand models wear a size 6½–7½ glove and a 4½–5½ ring, and have perfect skin without any visible veins. Male hand models wear a size 8½–10 glove, and their hands are classified according to shape. Male hands with long tapering fingers are used for glamor products and jewelry, while more utilitarian, rugged-looking hands are preferred for modeling household and outdoor items.

Female models with long, straight, shapely legs, proportionately long calves and slim ankles are hired for legwear, grooming products and shoes. Leg models work in television commercials as well as in advertising and editorial print. Feet that are slender, well shaped, carefully pedicured and a shoe size 6 are an added plus.

Parts modeling is a demanding profession. Trisha Webster, a very successful parts model with Wilhelmina, avoids the sun, housework and paper cuts. She does a daily manicure and pedicure, using a magnifying glass, to keep her hands

Body Parts Modeling

and feet in perfect condition. She has to wear gloves year round. Since a scar or disfigurement of any kind can permanently sabotage her career, Trisha's pampered nails, legs, hands and feet are insured by Lloyds of London for half a million

NEW LENGTHS
FRENCH MANICURE LACQUERS

Photo: Joe Neil/New Lengths French Manicure Lacquers

Photo: Michel Tcherevkoff/Diane Von Furstenberg

scream. Then I call the client or photographer for any upcoming bookings and explain the situation. That's only professional. It has never been a problem. If the left hand is blemished, we'll shoot the right one and transpose the film if necessary."

Trisha's body parts have appeared in hundreds of television commercials, ads, on billboards and on the cover of *Harper's Bazaar.* She also has an endorsement contract from Sally Hansen for nail-care products. Her advice for the individual who wants to get started as a body parts model is, "Make sure the part(s) you intend to market are photogenic. How would you like to see your foot in the pages of *Vogue,* enlarged several times its normal size? If that doesn't frighten you, parts modeling may be for you. At the same time, you may have lovely slender hands and feet or legs, but if they don't photograph well, then you can't hope to make a career in this specialty area. Test out your body part with simple snapshots or Polaroids. The skin should be smooth and the body part must appear graceful on film. So far so good? Now you can invest in some professional photographs, lit so as to enhance the body part. Lighting really does make a difference, so look carefully at a photographer's portfolio before hiring him or you'll waste time and money and still not

dollars! "I don't do any sports," says Trisha, "and I don't cook. My husband does all of these things for me. You could say I'm playing the role of the helpless female, but I don't see it that way. I consider myself a businesswoman. Modeling is a business—albeit glamorous—and can be a very lucrative one. But even with all the precautions I take, scratches do happen. The tiniest paper cut can be seen in a photograph. If I get a scratch I yell and get the photographs you need. Once you have some flattering photos, make copies and shop them around to the modeling agencies. Write your name, height, dress size, ring size, glove size, measurements and shoe size on the back of each photograph or have them printed up with this information typeset in a corner of the photograph."

The Fit Model

There is only one requirement for being a **fit model.** You must be the *exact size* a designer requires for his samples. That size varies from designer to designer. Some require a perfect size 6 or 8. Some cut a size 10. Designers also need "perfect sizes" for their petite and plus size lines. What is a perfect size? Well, that depends on the patterns a designer is using.

Some fit models are print models signed with an agency and doing fittings for extra money while they build their portfolios. But a fit model needn't have perfect features. She (or he) must simply be capable of maintaining her weight and measurements exactly.

The fit model's day can be long and monotonous, as she is pinned and sewn into outfit after outfit. But the financial rewards can make this type of work worthwhile. Fit models can make as much as $150 per hour.

Showroom Modeling

Showroom models are usually hired for a few days or weeks at a time during fashion market week, although some fashion houses hire models seasonally so that they have someone on hand to informally model the samples anytime a visiting buyer might be interested in seeing them. A showroom model must fit the majority of the samples a designer has created. She will model each outfit for the buyers visiting the showroom and recite the style numbers of the garments she is wearing when asked. The showroom model must be able to change quickly and show the clothing to advantage.

The size of a model chosen for a particular showroom depends again on the cut of the samples. While straight size 6/8 or 6–8 models 5'8"–5'9" are most in demand, petite models may be hired to show petite lines and plus size models to show the larger sizes. There is work for male models in showrooms that promote men's lines.

The rates for showroom modeling vary. Usually, a showroom model earns $200 to $1200 per day.

Campbell routinely stride down the runway topless and totally at ease. But not everyone can pull this off.

There is a difference between posing nude for a highly regarded, established photographer like Herb Ritts, Arthur Elgort or Bruce Weber, and disrobing for any photographer who asks. You can bet that a nude photograph by one of the professionals named will be of high standard and quality, will be printed *just so* and will not

Nudity and the Fashion Model

Only one rule applies: Listen to yourself. You must be comfortable with what you are doing. Most successful models are pretty comfortable with their bodies, clothed or unclothed. They understand that their face and body are the products to be marketed. However, there are top models, like Claudia Schiffer, who insist that under no circumstance will they ever pose nude. Others have made careers out of the attention they have recieved for their nude and seminude appearances in print. Supermodels Kate Moss and Naomi

appear *just anywhere.* These photographs have an intrinsic value and are highly regarded in the industry because of the talent and reputation of the photographer who shot them.

Of course, a photographer who is testing models and building a portfolio may well be capable of producing a quality photograph. It's the model's call. Do you trust this photographer? Have you seen enough of his or her work to feel comfortable posing nude? How will you feel if these photographs turn up in a second-rate publication in your hometown?

Here's another scenario: You are an established model, hired to do a nude photograph for a fragrance campaign. Your agent has shown you the layout for the ad, which will be shot by a leading photographer and which will appear in the world's foremost fashion magazines. Your agent has negotiated a contract that protects your rights, your image and pays you fairly for your work. You may feel more secure posing nude in a situation such as this—or *you may not.* Whatever the case, discuss your feelings with your agent. She (or he) should be willing to respect your wishes, at the same time suggesting career options best suited to your promotion as a model.

6 Modeling Opportunities in Foreign Markets

If you want to travel, modeling will give you plenty of opportunity to do so! Models building a portfolio will find that certain foreign markets offer excellent opportunities to work in editorial print. While these markets are competitive, they support a wide variety of quality fashion magazines and are open to experimenting with new faces. Beginning models are often sent abroad by their New York agents to gain valuable experience and tear sheets (editorial work published in fashion magazines). It is hoped that when a model returns from a foreign market her portfolio will be of such a quality as to be presented to American clients and fashion editors, increasing her chances of success and notoriety in the highly competitive New York market. It is not wise to attempt to break into any of the foreign markets without working closely with an agent in your own country. Your American agency must be able to communicate with an established agent in one of the major foreign cities, to see that you are properly promoted and protected.

The main editorial markets in Europe are the fashion capitals of Milan, London and Paris. But smaller markets, such as Madrid, are increasingly full of quality editorial opportunities. So is São Paulo, Brazil, Sydney, Australia, and some of the major Canadian cities also support some fine magazines and can be stepping-stones for the young model developing a look and a portfolio. The Canadian, British and Australian markets are good choices for the beginning model who is shy, very young or who might experience severe feelings of alienation in an unfamiliar environment. Because there is no language barrier (accents, however undecipherable, don't count), a young model, away from home for the first time, can gain some valuable experience without the panic of feeling (too) homesick.

Additional foreign markets offer catalog and advertising opportunities and the chance for models with a more commercial look to gain experience. These include Munich, Hamburg, Zurich, Vienna and Tokyo. Generally, the qualifications for modeling in all these cities approximate those for modeling in New York. Female models must be between 5'9" and 5'11" and a standard size 6–8 to work editorially and on the runway, 5'8"–5'10", size 6–8, for commercial print and catalog. The exception is Tokyo, where smaller models, 5'7"–5'8½", size 4–6, are sometimes preferred to fit the scaled-down samples of Asian designers.

The European markets, especially Milan and London, accept a

wider range of "looks" than are customarily marketable in the United States, although this too is changing. More extreme editorial models may find themselves much more accepted, at least initially, in the European forum. However, once a portfolio has been developed, many of these models find excellent opportunities in the New York market, which is increasingly experimenting with more exotic and unusual looks in its magazines and advertising. Take a look at Calvin Klein's campaign for the phenomenally successful fragrance CK1. You'll see a variety of young models, including Kate Moss, who hardly fit the stereotype model image. And other advertisers are following suit, following in Calvin's footsteps as they have since an adolescent Brooke Shields boasted, "Nothing comes between me and my Calvins" in the late '70s.

"If a model is very young, fifteen or sixteen," says Judy Linton, "I insist that a parent chaperone her first trip to Europe. That way, it is a learning experience, not only of modeling but also of growing within yourself. The influence of a parent helps. So much is new. It's another country. There's rejection to be dealt with—perhaps for the first time in a young person's life. A model must be given time to develop a coping mechanism to deal with rejection. I tell new mod-

els 'laugh about it.' But it is not always easy."

Let's take a closer look at some of the various markets.

Italy
Milan

Type of work available: Editorial, runway, television commercials, advertising
Rates: Editorial approximately $100–$250 per day. TV and advertising rates are negotiated by agents.
Currency: Italian lire (L)
Agency commission rate and taxes: 50 percent
Cost of living: Very high
Accommodations: $200–$250 per week (shared)

A model works in Milan for the editorial and runway opportunities. The city's central square, Piazza del Duomo, home of the beautiful Gothic cathedral, offers some relief from the otherwise gray cityscape, and you will find many of the city's current flock of young models gathered there on any given weekend, comparing notes and disturbing the pigeons.

So why do models even bother to

trudge it out in Milan, when the soulful beauty of other European cities beckons? Milan is the center of the Italian fashion industry. Armani, Valentino, Gucci, Prada, Versace—most of the great Italian designers are based here. Milan boasts a tantalizing array of high quality fashion magazines for the young model to peruse. And her chances of being featured in the editorial pages of one of them are better than in any other major market.

Even if a model works steadily in Milan, she will be lucky to cover her expenses and return home with a little pocket money. Rates in Milan are not very high, and the agencies take a whopping 50 percent in commissions and taxes. Furthermore, the cost of living is very high. The average model apartment or "pensione" costs $1600 to $2400 per month, so it is not unusual to find two or three models sharing a studio apartment.

When you plan a working trip to Milan, bring at least a month's rent with you (in traveler's checks), proof of medical insurance and spending money—enough for food and transportation for about two months. Even if you work immediately, your agency may take two or three weeks to issue you a check. It is a good idea to bring a credit card along, but don't expect to use it to pay for lodgings. Most Milanese apartments accept traveler's checks or cash only—and in advance, so be prepared. Men getting started in Milan should bring two months' rent along in traveler's checks. While men do work and build impressive editorial portfolios here, it may take them a little longer than their female counterparts to break into the market and actually begin to book work.

Some models find it difficult to make ends meet in this city. The low rates, combined with the high agency commission and taxes, and high cost of living can drain a model's funds very quickly. "Dancing for dollars," in which pretty girls are paid to dance on pedestals or with clients in the city's many nightclubs, is a common way for models to earn extra cash, but it is not recommended. It can negatively affect a young model's morale, and the late nights can take a toll on her performance as a model. Finally, the Milanese men are notoriously annoying to deal with. A young model may not possess the social skills and experience necessary to extricate herself gracefully from uncomfortable situations. Some models enjoy Milan's lively nightlife. Some get altogether carried away by it. Provided you keep your career goals in sight, you should be able to maintain a balance between work and play.

Traveling around the sprawling

city can be a frustrating experience for the uninitiated. Unlike the prompt and efficient German U-Bahn (subway), or even New York's somewhat less reliable subway system, the Metro and overland train systems of Milan seem to follow no set schedule. One is published, of course, but it's invariably ignored by conductors. The visiting model will soon learn to leave extra time for reaching bookings and appointments. Fortunately, clients are aware of the notorious lack of dependability with regard to scheduled travel and respond to slight tardiness with a characteristic shrug of the shoulders.

Americans may also find the drama of the Italian personality jarring at times. One young model, who happened to possess an ear for languages, began to pick up a good deal of Italian in her first few weeks in the country. To her astonishment, she found herself accused of actually being *fluent in Italian, but hiding the fact in order to make life difficult for her bookers!* For a girl (or guy) who takes these episodes seriously, modeling in Milan can be a culturally traumatic experience.

I recently got a phone call from Milan. A young model who had been there a month was in hysterics. She had options for several shows and a total of six television commercials. Unfortunately, every single option fell through. Out-

raged, the director of the Milanese agency screamed at her, accusing her of "wasting the bookers' time and efforts," of being "the most unlucky model the agency had ever taken on!" Understandably, she could no longer function with these agents. So I consoled her and made two phone calls—one to the agency director and one to the director of another agency in Milan. That afternoon the girl met with the second agent. She is currently working with the other agency, is much happier and is booking some very exciting work.

If you should have an unfortunate experience like the one just described, don't panic. Your career is not over. There are always options. Mere incompatibility with a foreign agent will not destroy your chances of working in that country. Your American agency should be there to support you and help you make the best of the situation.

Another model, unfamiliar with the Milanese practice of bargaining over the price of purchases, even in some of the better boutiques, relates this experience.

It was my second day in Milan. I had dropped my compact of pressed powder and it shattered. On my way to a go-see, I decided to buy another. I chose the least pricey looking shop in sight and went in. Nothing in the shop was ticketed. Of course, the clerk, a man, knew instantly that I was a model from America. I chose the most innocent looking powder compact I could find, not Chanel, or a brand name I recognized—and asked the price. The clerk replied with a smirk that it was 130,000 lire—over 100 American dollars!

I was so shocked that I just gave him my credit card and paid it! When I showed the compact to my booker at the agency, she shook her head and said it was worth less than $20. She explained that the Milanese bargain for items like this. For a long time after that I really dreaded having to purchase anything in that city.

—Kara L.

It takes time to develop the skill to know when and how to bargain for your purchases. The Milanese can be rather dramatic about it, turning it into a lively art form. But for the traveler unused to this practice, it can be intimidating. Bring everything you think you'll need to Milan. When you do buy something, try your hand at negotiating the price. You'll get good at it eventually, but until you do, try not to be too hard on yourself. And don't be afraid to walk out of a store if the price is too high. Sometimes this is the best bargaining tactic anyway—the clerk will often call you back in, offering the item to you at a more reasonable price.

Milan is a critical stop on the runway circuit, attracting models from all over the world for its show seasons, which are staged twice a year in February/March and September/October. An established model can make top dollar during show week, earning upwards of $5000 per show ($2000 for male models). Furthermore, if a model books shows directly from her New York agency, the higher European agency commissions can be avoided. For the beginning model, the shows in Milan are an excellent way to gain recognition in the business. Many a model has come to the notice of influential designers and booked prestigious print assignments as a result of her showcased runway appearances.

Great Britain

London

Type of work available: Editorial, runway, advertising
Rates: Editorial approximately

$100–$400 per day. Fees for shows and advertising rates are negotiated by agents.
Currency: British pounds sterling (£)
Agency commission rate: 20 percent
Cost of living: Very high
Accommodations: $175–$200 per week (shared)

Although the cost of living remains high in London, a model will keep more of what he or she makes. Agencies take a commission of 20 percent (25 percent if money is advanced before client payment). Models must be organized and professional. London is a good market for the serious beginner as there is no language barrier. Most of the work available is editorial and of a quality that is among the finest in the world. London is known for its lively, somewhat eccentric collections and groundbreaking editorial photography. British tear sheets can really make a model's portfolio stand out because of their photographic beauty and editorial slant.

The modeling industry in the United Kingdom has its own set of rules, laid down in *Terms, Conditions and Standards for Engagement of Professional Models in Still Photography*. This makes for a high level of professionalism and efficiency in the industry. Agents tend to be straightforward and honest.

Runway work is available for the shows held in February/March and October. American models traveling to London should bring with them at least $2000 in traveler's checks, proof of medical insurance and a return airline ticket.

We caught up with Wilhelmina model Tomiko in London, for a hands-on look at the British modeling scene:

What kind of work is available in London?

Europe as a whole has numerous magazines, so there is a lot of editorial work. As far as castings are concerned, they are pretty much the same everywhere. London is huge, so getting around is the biggest problem if you are new. Basically, you find the place, go in, you show your book, you have little conversation, if any, and then you wait to hear if you're booked for the job.

Describe a typical day.

I start my day at about 9:00–9:30, after plotting out my castings on the map. London is so big. In New York you can get to eight castings in a day. Eight castings in a day in London is really, really pushing it. So I would say my average has been five castings a day for the past two weeks, whether they be photographers or a magazine or a catalog client. You just go in, and like I said, you show them your book, talk to them, they'll ask you how long you are going to be here—because I'm not based in London, they want to see how long they have to use me. If they like me, they know I'm going to be here for two months. If I'm leaving next week, maybe they'll want to use me right away.

What's your London agency like?
I'm with Boss Models, and I started with them two weeks ago, and they are great. They are very supportive. They are very happy with the response that I've been getting. If I need anything, I have my booker's home phone number and home address. They know how it is to be so far away from home, so they want to make sure you have everything you need.

Even so, I'm already very homesick. It wears off after about a month, though. You just have to kind of set yourself up, give yourself the frame of mind to know that this is a job, and in order to do it well you have to make some sacrifices, and if sacrifice means being away from home for six weeks to three months, then you have to do that and make the best of it.

France
Paris

Type of work available: Editorial, advertising, runway
Rates: Editorial $100–$400 per day. Fees for shows and advertising are negotiated by agents.
Currency: French francs (Fr)
Agency commission rate and taxes: up to 67 percent
Cost of living: Very high
Accommodations: $150–$250 per week (shared)

Paris is the chic, glamorous, romantic home of some of the most dynamic design houses in fashion history—Chanel, Dior, Saint Laurent. The city is besieged by models from all over the world for the collections each year; haute couture in January and July, prêt-à-porter in March and September. The competition for spots on the runway is fierce, but French designers, eager to "discover" and mold new models, are happy to introduce a handpicked selection of fresh young faces on the catwalks each season. In order to work the collections, female models must be 5'9" or taller, with a maximum hip measurement of 34". Male models must be 6' to 6'2" and wear a size 40–42 suit.

Paris offers the beginning model valuable editorial opportunities. French fashion magazines like *Paris Vogue* are surpassed by none for the quality of their photography, art direction and printing. Tear sheets from these magazines make distinctive additions to a model's portfolio.

Every so often American television "news" and entertainment programs feature "exposés" on the fashion modeling industry in which they "uncover" all the dangers of the industry—the drugs, sex and scams. Paris seems to be the favorite target. It has been my experience that a young person who is troubled or unbalanced *will* get into trouble in Paris, in New York, in Milan, or for that matter, in his or her hometown. And a well-adjusted young person who is capable of keeping his or her goals in mind will skirt the dangers of any city, town or school quite neatly. If you are a person who is easily influenced by your peers, or who has a problem with drugs or alcohol, you might consider seeking counseling to gain some perspective on your life and activities before starting any new career, modeling included. My advice to concerned parents: Study your daughter's (or son's) lifestyle and habits. Discuss both

short-term and long-term goals in a nonjudgmental environment, enlisting the aid of an expert if need be. And don't blame Paris, or any other city, for an individual's choice of lifestyle.

Paris is an expensive city, comparable to Milan in the cost of food and accommodations. Watch where you take your coffee break—a coffee and croissant can run you up to $12 (American) in choice parts of town. A beginning model should bring at least $2000 in traveler's checks in order to live comfortably the first month. Buses, trains and the Métro offer efficient, reliable means of transportation around this breathtaking city.

Our traveling model overseas, Tomiko, gives us a first-hand look at the modeling industry in Paris.

How is modeling in Paris different from modeling in New York?
Well, I was shocked. I thought New York was the fastest city anywhere, but Paris is even more fast paced. I'd do eight or nine go-sees a day, from 9 A.M. to 8 or 9 P.M. Fortunately there are Métro stops every couple of blocks, so it's very easy to get around. Also, models can be more relaxed in New York. You can go on appointments wearing jeans and a T-shirt. In Paris, I was told by the agency to dress up. So I got really dressed up—like Jackie O. And when I went into the agency, they

said, "Oh no, no, you look too classy. We mean funky." It took me a while to catch on. Basically, anything trendy in basic black is right for Paris castings.

What kind of castings did you go on?
Oh, lots of shows because it was the season, and I saw some magazines and photographers. In the first ten days I did a show for Kenzo and an editorial story for *Madame Figaro*, which we shot in Texas.

What did you see of the city itself?
You see a lot just going on castings—you just bump into the sights by accident . . . the Champs-Élysées, the Arc de Triomphe, the Eiffel Tower. You're always walking by one of these landmarks. And I went out at night a couple of times, to some trendy places where industry people hang out—the Bains-Douche and the Bar Fly for dinner, and the Bus Line, which I equate to New York's Bowery Bar. So I had a good time. There's work in Paris and lots to see and do and it really is a beautiful city.

Spain
Madrid

Type of work available: Editorial, advertising, catalog, television commercials
Rates: From $200 per day for editorial to $1500 for catalog, advertising and television
Currency: Spanish pesetas (PTA)
Agency commission rate and taxes: 35–40 percent
Cost of living: Moderate
Accommodations: $125–$200 per week (shared)

Barcelona

Type of work available: Editorial, catalog, advertising, television commercials
Rates: $800–$1500 for catalog, advertising and television
Currency: Spanish pesetas (PTA)
Agency commission rate and taxes: 35–40 percent
Cost of living: Moderate
Accommodations: $125–$200 per week (shared)

Madrid and Barcelona may be a model's ideal introduction to the European market.

These less hectic cities are friendly grounds for the beginning model building a portfolio. They offer quality editorial opportunities as well as better paying catalog, television and advertising opportunities. This is the fastest growing modeling market in Europe. The cities themselves are delightful, with fine inexpensive restaurants, efficient means of transportation and near-perfect weather conditions. Barcelona, situated on the ocean, is a favorite weekend escape. The Spanish people are a joy to work with. They are eager to help a young traveler with directions or a menu translation. A visiting model will find herself booked on location assignments in nearby Spanish towns, many of them ancient walled cities overlooking the enchanting countryside.

The pensiones in which models stay in Spain are less costly than in some other European cities. Two models sharing an apartment will pay $500 to $700 per month each. Agencies take a 35–40 percent commission (taxes included) but, due to the variety of work to be booked in Spain, few models experience financial difficulties. Still, it is wise to bring $1500 in traveler's checks and proof of health insurance when you plan a working trip to Spain.

Germany
Munich and Hamburg

Type of work available: Some editorial but mostly catalog and advertising

Rates: Editorial $200–$600 per day; $1500–$2500 catalog and advertising day rate

Currency: Deutsche mark (DM)

Agency commission rate: 20 percent

Cost of living: Moderate

Accommodations: $75–$200 per week (billeted or shared)

Germany produces some of the biggest catalogs in the world. Models with commercial looks are in great demand. Much of the studio work is shot in Hamburg and Munich, while most of the location shoots take place in American cities, such as Miami and Phoenix. Many models work year after year for their German clients during catalog season and amass a considerable fortune. Rates are comparable to New York rates for catalog—$1500 to $2500 per day. German agency commissions are also competitive with American, at 20 percent.

Some editorial work is booked

out of Munich. *German Vogue* and *Elle* are headquartered there, and new faces are always welcome.

Both cities are easy to travel by bicycle or the very efficient underground (U-Bahn) systems. The cities are safe, and the business is possibly more low key and conservative here than in any other European market. Perhaps even more important for the beginner, nearly everyone in the industry speaks English. One tip for the model working in Germany: Do not be late for a go-see or booking! If it is a go-see, you will probably not be hired for the job. If it is a booking, you will not work for that client again. Lack of professionalism is grimly frowned upon by German clients. In fact, a model who does not show up for a confirmed booking can be held *liable for the day's production costs, including other models' fees!*

Agencies in Germany sometimes billet their models with families who have a room to rent. This is an inexpensive way to live as the participating families generally only charge $300 to $400 per month for a room and breakfast. Some models are lucky enough to make friends with the family and return to the same homes each year. Hotels in these cities can be expensive—from $80 per night upwards—so they are not recommended unless a model has definite advance bookings.

A tall commercial model with a girl-next-door healthy look will work almost immediately in these markets, usually booking work in the first two weeks. Still, it is best to arrive prepared, with about $1500 in traveler's checks and proof of medical insurance.

Switzerland

Zurich

Type of work available: Catalog
Rates: $1500–$2000 per day
Currency: Swiss franc (SF)
Agency commission rate and taxes:
   25–35 percent
Cost of living: Very high
Accommodations: $350–$600 per
   week (single occupancy)

As in the German market, catalog is the main fare in Zurich. Rates are comparable to those in Germany, but the agency commissions are generally 5 to 10 percent higher. Food and lodgings are very expensive. Models usually stay in the lower priced hotels, which run about $80 per night. Zurich does not have an underground, but the bus and tram systems are adequate. You will do a fair bit of walking, though, because many of the photographers have studios in their homes and those homes are often atop one of the city's surrounding hills.

Models planning an extended stay in nearby Milan often contact a Swiss agency to book them directly for the more lucrative catalog jobs. Such bookings can make building a portfolio in Italy much easier on the pocketbook. However, it is difficult for a beginning model to work in Zurich unless she is an exceptional commercial beauty. The Swiss expect a model to be professional, disciplined and experienced, and able to apply her own makeup expertly. An experienced model can arrive in Zurich with less than $500 as agencies here are more prompt in paying their models than anywhere else in the world. A model can, in fact, often collect her fee for a booking the very day the job is completed.

Austria

Vienna

Type of work available: Some editorial, advertising, catalog
Rates: Editorial $100–$200 per day; $1000–$1500 catalog and advertising day rate

Currency: Austrian schilling (S)
Agency commission rate and taxes: 20–30 percent
Cost of living: High
Accommodations: $150–$200 per week (shared)

Vienna is an excellent market for the model already working in the German-speaking countries. Most of the work available is advertising. Austrian clients prefer models with editorial looks for their advertising campaigns. Models with good portfolios will work immediately and steadily in this market, usually booking assignments in the week of their arrival.

Australia

Sydney and Melbourne

Type of work available:
Sydney—Editorial, advertising;
Melbourne—Catalog
Rates: Editorial $100–$400 per day; $1000–$1500 catalog; advertising rates negotiated by agents per assignment
Currency: Australian dollar ($A)
Agency commission rate: 20 percent
Cost of living: Moderate

Accommodations: $100–$150 per
week (shared)

Model's paradise? Some
think so. There is no
language barrier, the
attitude is laid back,
the weather good and weekends are
made for the beach. Plus the Australian fashion industry is booming.
Australia's fashion magazines are
now very professional, and there's
plenty of catalog work thanks to
Japanese clients who enjoy shooting
on location in the near perfect
climate. So start packing, but
remember that the seasons are
reversed, December being midsum-
mer.

Brazil
São Paulo

Type of work available: Editorial,
advertising
Rates: Editorial $60–$120 per day;
advertising rates negotiated by
agents
Currency: Cruzeiro (Cr$)
Agency commission rate and taxes:
20 percent
Cost of living: Moderate
Accommodations: $500 per month
(shared)

São Paulo is a great market
for the beginning model
because there are some
excellent fashion maga-
zines: *Vogue, Marie Claire, Elle.*
The quality of the photography is
comparable to the work in New
York and Paris. Men and women
with editorial looks will do best in
this market. An added bonus: Much
of the work is photographed on
Brazil's many beautiful beaches.

Japan
Tokyo

Type of work available: Catalog,
advertising, editorial
Rates: Fees are negotiated per
booking, by the agent, but
commonly exceed $1000 per
day
Currency: Japanese yen (¥)
Agency commission rate and taxes:
40 percent
Cost of living: Very high
Accommodations: $350–$450 per
week (single occupancy). Note:
Agency advances accommo-
dations as specified in the model-
agency contract.

The modeling agency system in Japan is unique. Models chosen by agencies are given contracts that usually span two months and guarantee the model a certain income during that time whether she works or not. By law, models must also receive prepaid round-trip airfare and accommodations. Payment is made at the end of the contract, before the model leaves the country, but models are advanced an adequate living allowance during their stay.

Models who have just arrived in Tokyo are usually driven around to go-sees by a driver hired by the agency until they become familiar with the city. Tokyo's train and underground systems are quick and efficient, with the names of stations written in both English and Japanese.

This is one of the few markets where a girl under 5'9" actually has an advantage. The Japanese samples run small. Consequently, models 5'7" to 5'8½" are preferred. A successful model in Japan can earn $30,000–$50,000 in a just few months—even if she is a beginner!

Canada

Toronto, Montreal, Vancouver

Type of work available: Editorial, advertising, catalog
Rates: Editorial $100–$400 per day; $1000–$1500 catalog and advertising day rates
Currency: Canadian dollar
Agency commission rate: 20 percent
Cost of living: Moderate to high
Accommodations: $125–$200 per week (shared)

The growing Canadian fashion industry is one distinguished by dedicated professionalism. Canadians are, for the most part, polite and efficient and expect the same from the models they hire. All three cities offer clean, easy-to-travel public transportation systems.

Travel Tips

Bring enough money! The number one complaint voiced by European agents is that American models arrive without enough money to pay their expenses until such time as they begin working. Depending on the market and on your particular look, you may book work immediately or it may take a month or more, so be prepared. To be on the safe side, have enough in traveler's checks to cover two months' rent and living expenses. This will make life in a foreign city more pleasant for you and keep your dealings with your host agency on a professional level. No one likes to beg an agent for advances—especially for work not yet booked. And agencies don't like to lend funds. In fact, most European agencies charge an extra 5 percent commission for doing so. Plan ahead and don't rely too heavily on your agent to provide for you.

Always keep your passport current and valid. You never know when a client may wish to book you for a direct assignment in a foreign country. You must be prepared to travel on a day's notice, or you could lose out.

Lose any excess weight *before* traveling to a foreign market. Don't expect that a change of environment will help you lose that extra 5 pounds. Foreign agents frown on overweight models. They might even refuse to send you out on go-sees until you lose weight. The cost of living, especially in the European markets, is very high. You don't want to sit around in a foreign city with the meter running.

Travel with at least $100 cash (including coins for telephones, etc.) in the currency of the country you are visiting. This will get you a taxi from the airport to the agency or to your hotel or pensione and allow you to purchase meals until you can arrange to visit a bank in the city of your destination.

Be sure to confirm the details of your accommodations before leaving home. Get the addresses and telephone numbers for the following: the hotel or pensione where you will be staying, your host agency and the home phone number of your booker, in case of delays or an emergency.

If you pack a blow-dryer, travel iron or other electrical appliance, remember to bring the electrical converters and plugs appropriate to your destination.

Bring along a sufficient supply of any medications you are taking. Some prescriptions can be difficult and costly to fill in foreign cities.

When flying, carry your portfolio and composites on board with you—not in your checked luggage.

7 Modeling Opportunities in American Markets

New York

Type of work available: Editorial, catalog, advertising, runway
Rates: Editorial $200–$400 per day; $1500–$2500 catalog day rate. Advertising and runway rates are negotiated by agency on a per assignment basis.
Agency commission rate: 20 percent
Cost of living: High
Accommodations: $125–$200 per week (shared)

New York is the most competitive market in the world. Its models command the highest rates, with top models earning about $200,000 per year. Supermodels with cosmetics contracts, fashion campaigns and product endorsements can make several million dollars per year. The standard for editorial is very high, and some of the world's best-known fashion photographers are based in New York.

While the cost of living in New York is relatively high, two or three models are usually housed in a model apartment. A model can expect to pay $500 to $700 per month in such an arrangement. Healthful, inexpensive food is easy to find in the city's numerous delis. Even restaurant food can be inexpensive, plentiful and delicious.

New York is, perhaps, the easiest large city in the world to travel. Many go-sees can be reached on foot or, increasingly, on in-line skates. The bus and subway systems make it possible to reach any appointment within forty-five minutes (unless the train or bus breaks down). Taxis are still inexpensive when compared to those serving the major cities in Europe, but traffic jams make public transportation preferable if time is a factor.

The tents in Bryant Park (nicknamed Seventh on Sixth) are home to the New York collections, staged in April and November. These are, increasingly, a draw for models from all over the world. Rates for shows are very high. A top female model can make upwards of $5000 per show (male models, $2000), with supermodels cashing in at $15,000!

Miami

Type of work available: Catalog
Rates: $1200–$2500 catalog day rate
Agency commission rate: 20 percent
Cost of living: Moderate to high

Accommodations: $150–$175 per week

Miami is the catalog capital of the fashion industry. Its predictably fine weather has lured clients from Germany, France and Italy. The city and coastline are turned into back-to-back sets for fashion shoots during the busiest season, September through February. Models from all over the world fly in and out of Miami to take advantage of the consistent and well-paid catalog work available. At these times hotels are packed with photo crews, so it may be difficult to find accommodations for the model not directly booked on assignment. Plan ahead with your Miami agency when visiting to meet clients for the first time.

Los Angeles

Type of work available: Catalog, editorial
Rates: Editorial $200–$400 per day; $1500–$2500 catalog day rate
Agency commission rate: 20 percent

Cost of living: Moderate to high
Accommodations: $175–$200 per week

Many top models whose ambitions run to film and television have chosen to make Los Angeles their home base. As a result, the L.A. market is nearly as competitive as New York's. There are models in abundance, vying for a limited number of opportunities. Models beginning their careers in Los Angeles will usually be sent to Europe to build editorial portfolios before being sent to the major clients in L.A.

San Francisco

Type of work available: Catalog
Rates: $1500–$2000 per day
Agency commission rate: 20 percent
Cost of living: Moderate to high
Accommodations: $150–$200 per week

Catalog clients are attracted to the beauty of San Francisco and by its ideal climate. The city is the perfect place for new models to gain some experience without the stress of the major markets.

Dallas

Type of work available: Catalog
Rates: $1500–$2000 per day
Agency commission rate: 20 percent
Cost of living: Moderate to high
Accommodations: $150–$200 per week

Dallas is a growing market, with plenty of catalog opportunities for the beginning model. It is also an excellent market for male models.

Chicago

Type of work available: Catalog, advertising, television commercials
Rates: $1500–$2000 per day
Agency commission rate: 20 percent
Cost of living: Moderate to high
Accommodations: $150–$200 per week

Cindy Crawford, one of the highest paid models in the world, got her start working with Chicago's reigning photographer, Victor Skrebneski. The Chicago market is ideal for the beginner. The second largest market in the United States, Chicago offers a range of modeling opportunities. Standards are high, and models are expected to be professional. While most of the work is catalog, Chicago provides a good training ground for new models, and its agencies are eager to groom young stars for the more competitive markets.

Phoenix

Type of work available: Catalog
Rates: $1250 per day
Agency commission rate: 20 percent
Cost of living: Moderate
Accommodations: $150–$175 per week (shared)

Phoenix is a growing market, with plenty of catalog opportunities for the beginning model.

8 THE **M** ALE MODEL

The male model's time has come! Never before have male models enjoyed such attention and publicity. These men are in a position to rival the female supermodels as celebrity figures, heros and icons of a generation. It really is an exciting time for men in fashion.

Most male models are 6'0" to 6'2" and wear a size 40–42 suit. Standard measurements are chest 38–40, waist 32–34, and inseam 32–34. But there is room for exceptions. Advertisers are exploring more unusual looks in attempts to create distinctive, eye-catching campaigns. Some very successful male models have wiry frames rather that the classic muscular (but not overly built up) silhouette. Shorter men or very tall men may find work in commercial print and television. Men who wear a size 44 long suit can take advantage of opportunities in the men's big and tall market.

Male models take their work very seriously. They know they must stay in shape; therefore grooming, fitness and diet routines are carefully followed. Like female models, male models have their hair cut by the top stylists in New York, Paris and Milan. Light weight lifting for strength and endurance, in-line skating, swimming, running and group sports like basketball and soccer are among the favorite

Photo: Rodney Smith/W magazine

GIORGIO ARMANI

Photo: Peter Lindbergh/Giorgio Armani

cardiovascular exercises. Most male models are careful to get enough sleep, because lack of sleep does affect appearance, for

Photo: Peter Lindbergh/DKNY Hollywood

men as well as for women.

A low-fat diet is preferred, but many guys admit that they "cheat a lot on the type of food—just not too often."

Wilhelmina agent Sean Patterson represents top male model Mark Vanderloo. Together, they are credited with breaking many of the rules that have long been applied to men in the industry and paving the

way for a new, more powerful generation of male models. Mark's yearly earnings exceed the totals of many of the female supermodels, proving some guys can make the big bucks. Mark is also the first male model to do several major print campaigns for top designers, such as Calvin Klein and Donna Karan, that ran simultaneously in the magazines!

Mark was born in the hamlet of Waddinxveen, the Netherlands. At twenty-two, he entered the University of Amsterdam to study history. One day, he accompanied his model girlfriend to a shoot. The photographer liked him instantly and hired him for an ad for milk. A local agency loved the photographs and took him on as a client. In June 1992, Mark signed with Wilhelmina Models and soon found himself doing upscale print work and major runway shows—for Armani, Valentino, Trussardi. Calvin Klein chose him for the fragrance Eternity, with Christy Turlington. Hugo Boss and Donna Karan hired him for print campaigns and runway appearances every chance they got. In fact, Donna Karan was telling everyone that Mark Vanderloo was her "favorite model of all time."

Supermodel status evolved quickly into celebrity status. Mark was asked to do interviews with *Agency* and *Max* magazines in

Paris, and *Arena* in London. That led to television shows and specials featuring Mark as a guest or guest host—among them, appearances on E! Entertainment TV and the *Today* show.

What's Mark got? Even Sean, his agent, can't quite put his finger on it.

I am his agent, and I know there is something untouchable about this kid, [but] even I can't come up with it. You will sit there, and you will just naturally be attracted to the guy. He just has such a charisma, such an unbelievably real-person charm—coupled with winning the lottery of the gene pool, you know—happening to be a great-looking guy doesn't hurt. And he's the consummate professional. You can't *not* like the guy! He makes you laugh.

He started booking work right away—the best stuff. When that happened, we thought, Well, let's see how this goes, and let's manage him correctly. You know, image control, only the best jobs, the best campaigns. Well, the thing about Mark is that about a year and a half ago—it was the most unbelievable thing in this industry, because before Mark came along, you would do basically one campaign, you didn't do the other campaigns. Armani did not want Donna Karan's models showing up and vice

versa. Mark did every stinking campaign. He did Armani, Valentino, Trussardi, Trussardi fragrance. The next season got even bigger. In the fall, his newest set of campaigns came out. He did the Hugo Boss campaign. He did the Calvin Klein Eternity campaign. He did the Donna Karan campaign. He did just everything—and, believe it or not, Donna Karan herself is pushing him for movies right now! That's the kind of effect he has on people. I can bring you video tapes where Mark's done interviews for the *Today* show, or E! Entertainment television, or for NBC, and Donna would be interviewed and she'd say like,"No, you don't understand, this guy's incredible—and if anyone wants Mark for a movie, just call me!" And this was after all of his campaigns came out for Calvin Klein Eternity and Calvin Klein Menswear and all of that.

You realize when you hear these things that there is an underlying charm and charisma and likability about Mark. I think designers are willing to allow it—allow Mark to model other designers' campaigns, even competitors', because he creates such a great image for each of them. I tend to think that we, as his agents, have had something to do with protecting that image, making sure his level of visibility in only the best campaigns is as high as possible. He is an anomaly in this industry right now. We have broken so many barriers with this kid in so far as we have made it acceptable for clients to pay some phenomenal amounts of money for men!

Not surprisingly, Sean is enthusiastic about the changes in the men's fashion industry and excited about his role promoting male models in this ever-expanding forum.

Obviously the changes are such a part of my life—seeing what happened with Mark. A lot of guys want to come with Wilhelmina because they hope to be the next Mark Vanderloo. Now don't get me wrong, we have a lot of great images in here, great guys. And anybody would want to have the career of any one of these guys. I've been in and around the industry for the past five years. While the men haven't yet, as a whole, caught up with the women, certain men are, in a very short time, breaking down the barriers. There are a few guys right now who are kind of like A– supermodels. Some are making as much if not more than the top girls on the jobs they book. It's nice to see. Certain female supermodels are household names—you know the ones. Well, you'll see male models become that recognizable, for a variety of reasons—one of which is that it has become more sociably acceptable

for men to acknowledge other good-looking men, a guy can acknowledge his own looks and try and improve himself—his looks and just everything about him. It's nice to see that people are finally able to appreciate all sorts and forms of beauty, whether it be male or female.

Men are landing lucrative contracts, which act as a tremendous boost to their careers. But you also need the campaigns going on from season to season. The guys, for example, who have fragrance contracts, whether they be exclusive or not, can always still do the clothing campaigns from season to season. And some of these guys get five or six campaigns a season and can make—especially the guys who are competing with the women—well, $15,000 to $20,000 a day is not unheard of. I've seen some of these guys walk home with more for a three-day campaign than I know I'll make in two or three years. So I guess that kind of puts it into perspective.

The look for male models is changing as well—advertisers are more willing to experiment. Men with unusual or less-commercial features are becoming more appealing, especially to cutting-edge designers who want to have distinctive-looking campaigns. Sean explains.

I think that fashion is at a crossroads right now. You have these photographers and clients looking for different types of guys. Your Steven Meisels, your Shotoshis and your Steven Kleins want offbeat and quirky guys. But, overall, advertisers are for the most part still looking for great-looking, healthy people.

I think that at the end of the day, when Calvin goes to his meeting with his advertising agency, and Donna goes to the meeting with her advertising agency, they are faced with the fact that they have to move suits—70 to 80 percent of the menswear industry is still suits. Everybody has to have something to wear to work. Donna, Calvin—they all have to move this clothing. And if they want to do that, they are going to have to find models who can appeal to that thirty-five-year-old businessman and his wife. So there is a certain advantage to being classic looking. These men can have careers that last well into their forties. We have quite a few guys in here. Bruce Hulse was a huge model, and he still makes a fortune.

What does Sean look for in a male model?

For a male model to be successful, some obvious things come to mind. Be on time. Be professional. Have a neat appearance. I advise the younger models who come in to pick up fashion magazines, read them. Pay attention to what's going on in the industry. See which photographers are shooting which kinds of editorial. See who the clients are using and why. How does all of it apply to you? Where do you fit in? What are your strong points? It doesn't do anybody any good to walk into any situation blind. It just makes sense to educate yourself.

Of course, Europe is a great training ground for the beginner. Basically there are two major markets—New York and Paris. Milan absolutely, positively has a place and would be arguably the third major market crucial for models. And I would say there are a bunch of secondary markets, including London, Miami, Los Angeles, Germany. But the major three are New York, Paris and Milan. They all have a different place right now in regard to the male-model industry. In Milan, you build up your book—get editorial tear sheets. Any advertising job you do in Milan, for the most part, is going to pay a lot less money than you'd make in New York or Paris. Then again, the designers in New York and Paris aren't going to want to use you until they see those Milanese tear sheets—until they see that Italian editorial—a few Italian campaigns. So in a way, Milan is ahead of us. Everyone likes to know what Giorgio Armani is doing, or Versace—who they're using in their campaigns. But it's definitely a world market, and you can't exist, at least in the realm of high fashion, unless you keep on moving. If you're not moving, you are finished. If you're a young guy and you're twenty-four years old and you have a great book from Milan but you just stay there [while] the other guys are going to Paris and New York as well, and they're meeting and working with all those clients—it's making them more attractive to everybody. It's not good for a career to sit in any one city for too long. Some of these guys are on planes every two days. I remember last year I had one who had a string of eight consecutive weeks where he was on a plane at least three times a week. So that's twenty-four flights in eight weeks. It's unbelievable. They definitely do earn these exorbitant salaries sometimes, you know. There is an argument to be made for how much work they do actually put into it. It is not as easy as it looks. I think [there] is a misconception that these models, you know, their lives are so easy—let's take a few pictures and smile for the camera—and that's not necessarily true. Nor does it happen overnight. You have to build up tear sheets, put in time in all the markets, and then it's only one job that puts you over the top, one booking that gets you the worldwide recognition.

A lot of these guys are not making much money at first. Many times, I've lent money out of my pocket to a model—$10 so he could eat that night. We try very hard to take care of our models. We put them in a model apartment. We try to make sure that they are okay, that they have adequate everything. Still, it isn't any fun living in any of these major cities when you only have $10 in your pocket. And for a lot of these guys the first few months are very much like that. We wind up trying to get them part-time jobs in the meanwhile, to get them through. For us it's reaffirming—it makes us feel confident if they are willing to get a job, because it shows us that they do understand that there is a level of work and commitment involved, and that it isn't supposed to be a free ride. The Cinderella story really doesn't exist. It's like anything else, if it's worth having, it's worth working for.

Supermodel Mark Vanderloo

I t's little wonder that Mark Vanderloo is the world's most sought-after male model. Besides having an irresistible look, Mark's personality is one of charm and humor. He looks you right in the eye when you're talking and peppers his speech with beguiling grins and winks. Here, Mark shares the secrets of his success.

One of the outstanding things about your career so far is that you've broken through some of the barriers that men face in the industry, like appearing simultaneously in campaigns running for designers as influential as Calvin Klein and Donna Karan. What has allowed you to do this?

If you are starting out and you work for one client that season—let's say I did the Giorgio Armani campaign—then what you are is the "Giorgio Armani Kid." . . . You get labeled, and no one will touch you after that, because you are identified with that designer or product. Well, I was pretty lucky, because when I started doing campaigns that first season—I

DKNYHOLLYWOOD

Photo: Peter Lindbergh/DKNY Hollywood

had like six different campaigns out: Valentino, Trussardi, Donna Karan, Oliver, etc. I couldn't be identified with a single campaign. But you have to keep all those clients happy! So I tried to give every client their very own image.

If you put the campaigns next to each other—it's the same guy, but there are different styles, different concepts, different looks and different photographers. You know, you can get that funky feeling, you can have a moody feeling, you can get a relaxed feeling. So Valentino is very happy; they thought they had the most beautiful campaign. Giorgio Armani is very happy. He thought he had the most beautiful campaign. Trussardi, Donna Karan—each is unique. Each felt they got the very best.

What's the best thing about modeling?

I think the best thing about modeling is that anyone who is successful is able to step up the social ladder in life, more or less. If you are born in a trailer, and your whole family lives in a trailer, and you're very beautiful and become a model, you have the opportunity to make some money and create a different lifestyle for yourself—for your family, even. And if you are smart, you can maintain it. Basically, you are rewarded for something that has to do with a combination of skill and appearance. You don't have to be beautiful, either. There are ugly models, both male and female, who do very well. I think the better pictures are made by a good feeling rather than simply by a pretty face.

You mentioned the word "smart." What makes a model smart?

A smart model can cope with all the different kinds of people that you encounter in the business—all the egos. And you know your way around; you feel comfortable as you are in various situations. But initially when I said the word "smart" I meant smart with money. If you have $1000 coming in, you can spend it on an upgrade for first-class, or you can say, "You know what, I'm going to put $500 in the bank and give $500 to my mom." If you have so much money coming to you, then you should spend it in a way so as not to waste it. A lot of models do waste it. They make a lot of money and the first thing they do is buy a beautiful car. The money is gone. And they forget about having to pay insurance and parking and everything else that goes with it, so they have to maintain all the costs that go with the spending. And that's not smart.

Especially if you're traveling two hundred days a year . . .

Yeah, that's a waste. You know, you're better off saying, "Okay, I'm going to invest somewhere." Do a little research into some safe places to keep your money.

What advice would you give a model just starting out?

First, take a look at the magazines.

See where you fit in. Know your strong points and where you can and should be working. You get the models who work for magazines and it's great. They work for magazines all the time. It's beautiful. But they don't really make a lot of money. Or you've got models who only work for catalogs. They make a lot of money but they don't really work for the magazines, you know. So you get different types of models within the same industry. And I think it is up to you to determine what you want to do and what you're capable of doing. The first time I went to Milan, I ran into a friend of mine—this guy is Dutch too. He was completely down. The kid was working in Amsterdam—doing a lot of catalog. He was making a lot of money. He was making ten grand a month. It was pretty good, no problem. And I said, "Why didn't you just stick to what you are doing, because that's where you are making money?" But he wanted the magazines. He was aiming for something that didn't work out, and he got depressed over it. He had no idea what his strengths were—or his limitations. First you have to be confident within yourself. And you have to deal with rejection. You have no idea what a client wants. You walk into a casting, and they basically ignore you—and you don't book the job. You feel that they don't like you. Well, that's not the case. They have a need to fulfill; maybe your hair is dark and they want blond hair. Or maybe your eyes are blue and they want brown eyes. You have no clue. So you can't take it personally. But it's hard in the beginning—you get depressed over it because you think they don't want you. At the very start you should see yourself as a product. You try to make sure the product is as good as possible. Take care of yourself, your health, your appearance. You take care of your clothing. You dress well. And, as I said, prepare yourself. Do some research so you can get the maximum out of your presence. Distance yourself a little. When I look at my pictures, it's not me. It's very funny. I'm looking at a guy in a picture—who should improve this, that and the other. That's how I look at myself—at those images.

What about education?

Oh, definitely finish high school. Without my basics in school I wouldn't get around as easy as I can. And I still feel that I haven't educated myself enough. I went to university for a year. I'm not under-educated, but I still have plenty to learn. And the more you see, the more you know you don't know anything. That's really sad to find out when you are twenty years old—and you've seen the whole world—but fast, you know. It kind of flew by you and your head is still spinning.

You waste your youth, and no job is worth your education, your youth, your partying with your friends, because that's where you get your power from. That's what you can relate to later. I think you shouldn't jump into modeling. It doesn't really matter if you start when you're thirteen or seventeen, eighteen—you're still young. If you are going to make it, you're still going to make it. Everyone should finish their education first. I'm very happy I had my languages in school. I speak five languages, and it sure helps when you're traveling.

What is the lifestyle of the working model?

Well, it depends where you are in your career. There are several stages you go through. For example, when you start out modeling everything is new for you. You come to a new city, and you live in a hotel, and you don't understand the language, and you're sent around and it's difficult to find wherever you have to go—you're thrown in the deep end, basically. So you grow up quickly. It's like throwing a kid in the pool to learn how to swim. You have to do something because otherwise you sink. But it gets crazy. I just took my first vacation in three years.

Where did you go?

Spain, Ibiza. I took little bits of everything. Little bits of rest, little bits of going to the beach, hanging out with friends. And I didn't call anybody—didn't have a phone around.

Sean [Mark's agent] told me he practically had to order you to take some time off.

Well, yes. At some point it is really necessary to take a vacation, because you forget—you just run on and on. You think—I don't need a vacation if I do a trip [working] to the Caribbean for ten days, it's fine. But it isn't fine, you know, because you are waking up at six o'clock every morning and you're still working ten hours a day. You don't have time to sleep even if you need to sleep. So the lack of sleep and the amount of traveling really catch up with you—wear you down.

Sounds like a lot of work and very little play . . .

It's just how you treat it. Everybody has a different schedule. Everybody has different needs. Everybody thinks differently. I know models whose life is a holiday. They have a holiday all year round and once in a while they work. They work eighty days a year or whatever—which is actually pretty good for a model. But if you're really busy, you can't take it. You can't go out and party all night, which I used to do. I used to party all night and go to the studio the next day, no problem. But that lifestyle is going to get you—especially if you fly a lot internationally. I live in perpetual jet lag, so I can't run out at night and party on. It's not worth the price you're going to pay the next day.

Sometimes you get tired of moving so fast . . .

Yes. That part's tricky. You may be building some financial stability, and that's great. But you have no steadiness in your life. Your hours are never the same. I just came from London yesterday, and I'm in New York now, you know. It's normal, for me. I don't have my breakfast at eight o'clock every morning. I don't have my dinner every night at the same time. Eventually you need some kind of stability—so I'm looking for a place in New York. I've been traveling so much over the last couple of years, and I don't have a home anywhere. So I think it's important for me to set up a base—to settle in. I would like to work on an acting career too—and maybe do some kind of team sport every week. I look forward to doing something normal—cook a meal maybe! Over the last three years I've cooked maybe ten meals. I don't have a kitchen because I live in hotels. You might think, "Wow! I wish I could eat in restaurants all the time." I don't enjoy restaurants anymore. I'd like to have my basics set. And then I think I have to rest in my body. I'm sort of a nervous person, always here and there, always running around. I think I should straighten out my head first.

Then I'll have the peace of mind to concentrate on acting and go for that. You can't just jump off the plane and jump into acting.

How did you feel when you landed the Calvin Klein campaign for Eternity?

I felt very satisfied. I'm very fortunate in what I'm capable of doing. When I started modeling and the first time I went to Milan—I looked at all the magazines. What can I do? Where do I fit in? And I was looking at the pictures for Armani. I might be able to do an Armani campaign, I thought. I'm sort of the type of guy Armani uses. And when that day came, I was so happy. I had already shot the Valentino campaign, which I never expected because they always shoot dark-haired guys. I shot the Trussardi campaign, which I had considered as a possibility. So I was really very content with how my career was going. By the time I got Calvin Klein, I'd been working for a while already, and I already had a lot of happiness in my career. For me the best thing about Eternity was that I was working with Christy Turlington. She's a very special person.

You've worked on so many major campaigns. Is there a dream assignment that you have in mind? Or have you done it all?

I guess I'd like a $5,000,000 contract. I'm just kidding here.

I'm told you are getting close. You're getting paid more on some bookings than the top female models you are working with. Are the rates beginning to even out for men and women?

They are improving, but at the end of the day it's not going to stay. Just look at women's magazines and the women's industry. There is still a thin layer of top girls . . . I think there is no doubt that the girls' rates are set. As for the men, there are still so many agents selling out, and that's basically the problem. Also, there are so many more products for women; it's a much bigger market. I'm not asking for the same or more.

What about show rates?

It all depends—on the show, the designer, the model. I like doing shows. I like to see what the designers come up with each season. But it is the hardest work—it keeps you busy for four weeks, and you do fifty shows—and at the end of show month you are not exactly going home with a big bag of money. You're making enough, but it's not like the girls. They can rake in like a hundred grand during show season, whereas we can make $40,000.

What advice would you give the beginning model?

If you are starting out as a model, then it is very important to go with the right agent. You need the break in the beginning, and if they push you and have the right contacts, they can make everything work for you. It makes a big difference. Then again, you have to sort out for yourself which agency is best for you. My agent here at Wilhelmina, Sean Patterson, is great for me, but maybe not for some other guy. He believes in me, and I, in him.

You should have a good rapport with your agent. There are agents I would never trust. I would never want to be represented by P. J. from R. Agency—and yet he is a very good agent. I don't like the guy, and maybe he doesn't like me.

When you start out, work where your market is best and where you're happy. Your success depends greatly upon how you feel about yourself. If you feel good in Italy, work in Italy. If you feel like crap there, you aren't going to work, because that attitude is going to show. It's going be apparent to the agent when you come in grumpy every day, and he [the agent] will say, "I'm not going to send him to any clients." So you have to understand what you are feeling, what you want to do and what you are capable of doing. Know which league you are going to be playing in and how far you're going to take it.

Michael Bergin

You know Michael Bergin from the Calvin Klein underwear ads and for his acting debut on CBS's *Central Park West*.

In 1993, Calvin Klein began searching for a model to represent his underwear line and replace rapper Marky Mark. He chose Bergin to appear both alone and with Kate Moss in the new campaign. The ads appeared all over the world, making Bergin a recognizable top model almost overnight. Since then, Bergin has become a favorite on the runways of top designers, including Calvin Klein, Donna Karan, Giorgio Armani, Hugo Boss, Valentino and Trussardi. He has also done several additional print campaigns and television commercials for Coty Exclamation! fragrance, Maybelline, Kellogg's and Bacardi rum. Here, he shares with us some of his thoughts about the business and his experience as the "Calvin Klein Guy."

Michael, how did you get started in the business?

Well, I wasn't spotted by Bruce Weber [photographer] walking on the beach. I was going to school—University of Connecticut—and a few friends and relatives suggested I try modeling, so I looked into it. There are modeling schools in Connecticut, where I live, but all they wanted was my money. Well, it sort of turned me off, so I went back to school for another year, and then the next thing you know summer is here again. The son of a friend of my father's used to model in New York. He gave me some tips and informa-

Calvin Klein
underwear

Photos: Tiziano Magni/Calvin Klein Underwear

Photo: Aldo Rossi/Paloma Picasso Ctee Minotaure

tion. He said, "Everything is in New York. If you are living in Connecticut, the closest market is New York. It's a big market. You should find an agency in New York." He gave me a list of agencies. So one day I went out searching for agencies in New York, and I found this small agency. And they gave me the name of a photographer I should see. I set up an appointment, came back to New York and tested with him. And he called up Click [Model Management] and said, "I got a guy you might be interested in." He sent me over there, and Click took me in and started sending me out. But I was still

going to school, so I was commuting back and forth and doing the best I could with my studies and going to castings. But it was very difficult. So I waited till I graduated, and then I moved out to New York. I had to get it off my chest—had to actually try it—see for myself that *it wasn't going to work out.* When I moved out to New York I switched to Wilhelmina.

How did you feel when you got the Calvin Klein account?

I didn't know quite how prestigious and how big a thing it was going to be. I mean, it really changed my life! I was familiar with the Marky Mark ads, but he's a celebrity. So I didn't think I was going to get the same exposure and publicity as he did. And I'm not saying I did, but I came pretty close.

So that campaign really changed your life—put you over the top as a model . . .

Without a doubt, yes. I'd done a few campaigns here and there, some fashion, some fragrances, this and that, but I'd only been at it a year and a half. There are many guys in the business that are so popular—those guys are like supermodels. They've done every designer campaign possible. I haven't been in the business long enough to have had that kind of recognition. You see, the Calvin Klein campaign kind of made me. But the exposure was so great that no one else wanted to use me for a while. People just saw me as the Calvin Klein guy. It was not an exclusive contract—but it's had that effect. The phone was ringing off the wall. Every newspaper, magazine, TV segment—everyone wanted to know who this new guy was, know a little bit about him, and for the last year and a half that's what I've been doing. I've been keeping busy doing a lot of publicity. And I don't even have a publicist. I've never sought out any of it. I became more and more well known, and here I am today. I'm the same person today, but things are a little bit different.

How are they different?

Well, people recognize you. I'm not like looking around to see if people are recognizing me. But at times people will scream out "Michael! Hey, Calvin Klein!" Things like that. It does give you a good feeling. I probably would hate it if I were being chased down the street, but it's nice for people to recognize you, and they respect your space. They just say "hello," and walk on.

You're doing the shows too. How do you like that?

I used to hate doing the shows because I was always nervous. And the anticipation—designers will have you at the show four hours before the thing starts, and I would just freak out! What do you do for four hours? They probably have a fifteen-minute rehearsal in that time. And I was new, and I didn't know all these other guys—twenty-five other guys, and they were all really good-looking, great bodies and popular. And once on the runway—everybody staring—well, it took some getting used to. I knew this was what I had to do. But it sure took the fun out of doing the shows, for a while anyway. But once I became the Calvin Klein image, I felt more confident. I was able to shake some of that nervousness—I'll never shake all of it. I was able to enjoy the shows and have fun with it. By then I knew a lot more of the guys, if not all of them. Now I love it, just trotting down the runway. It's fun.

Photo: G. Bruckheimer

What advice would you give to someone just starting out in the business?

Just take it day by day. Try to experience and learn the best you can. For example, I don't beat myself up for things I don't get, because I don't expect them. But if I do get something, it's celebration time!

What do you do to relax?

Besides sleeping? I love to like walk around. I like shopping. I never really buy anything. Most of the time I just like to look. I love to look. I run. I exercise—at the gym doing a Stair-Master, or outside running down the West Side Highway. I've been playing basketball a lot, and I've been Rollerblading a lot. These are things I enjoy doing that get your mind off everything. I try to keep my composure and not get freaked out—because a lot of the stuff I've been doing I can't believe I'm doing. Growing up, I was this shy little kid. I always ran away from the camera—totally camera shy.

Photo: Troy Word

How do you feel in front of the camera now?
A little bit better.

A little bit?
Well, a lot better. There is

always going to be this nervousness inside of me—the camera looking at you—but now I can use it to my advantage. It just makes me more creative. I have a lot to offer, and I think that's why acting will also become a passion of mine. So it's not just about my face, not just about my body, but it's about my personality too, about me inside—that I can show people.

You've already made a start acting . . .

Yes, I'm getting quite involved. I've got a recurring role on *Central Park West*. I'm not great at it yet, but I feel it, and I like it a lot. I'm taking classes, and I'm going on readings. I was in a Vanessa Williams video. I played her drunken fiancé. It was fun. I really had to act that part. The director was very pleased. That gave me real confidence. And two weeks ago I shot a little part in my first film, it's a Merchant-Ivory film called *La Proprietaire*. It was fun. All in one summer, I was a D.J., host of a music video show, had a couple of parts in a TV series and was involved in a film. Plus the shows and the whole modeling thing. There's a lot going on, and as much as it is stressful and there is a lot of pressure, it's what I want to do. I want to be busy, and I want things to keep happening.

9 ETHNIC MODELING

The opportunities for ethnic models, whether they be black, Asian, Hispanic or Native American, are expanding dramatically as we move away from rigid ideas about beauty. Models of all colors are appearing in the most highly sought after editorial spreads in fashion magazines eager to create impact and unforgettable images. Ethnic models are gracing the catwalks of the top designers and landing lucrative cosmetics contracts, fragrance and fashion campaigns. Nonetheless, some clients still insist upon the "all-American" look. This is all the more peculiar, because it has traditionally meant a northern

Photo: Pablo Ramirez

Photo: Dick Nystrom

European or Scandinavian look—blond, blue-eyed; not American at all. Slowly, this is changing. Think about it: ten years ago, supermodel Christy Turlington would have been labeled "ethnic."

Judy Linton emphasizes: "Gone is the tokenism—of one black girl or one Eurasian, one Hispanic or one Chinese. There are more Europeans appreciated here, because there are all different sorts of people buying magazines today. And the designers have opened that market, so you find that, on the whole, people are accepting the beauty of the blue-eyed blonde and the beauty of the dark-eyed Asian equally. Wilhelmina alone has over sixteen ethnic models who command salaries of over $175,000 per year. Since I have been involved in the industry, this is the easiest time ever for models of color."

Kevin Jones believes that Janice Dickinson opened a lot of doors in the industry by being "the first dark superstar—a dark-haired girl with a certain panache." Models could now be noticed for creating something special on film. Now we have all different types of top models: Claudia Mason, who is of mixed parentage; Ariella, who is Dutch and Japanese. We have Vietnamese girls doing the Revlon campaign!

There's a whole range of looks. Now everyone can identify. Everyone can look in a magazine and say, "That's me! That could be me!"

Beverly Johnson

Wilhelmina supermodel Beverly Johnson made history in August 1974 by becoming the first black model to appear on the cover of American *Vogue*. Since then, Beverly has graced numerous covers and has added acting and writing credits to her list of achievements. Beverly has written an informative, insightful guide to health and beauty for women of every age and color entitled *True Beauty*. In its pages are discussed many of the questions and concerns facing the ethnic model, including special beauty routines for ethnic skin and hair.

Here, Beverly shares her experiences as a model and her hopes for the future.

How did you get started as a model?

I was going to school at Northeastern University. There weren't any summer jobs, and I came to New York. I had an appointment at *Glamour* magazine, and they liked me . . . simple as that.

How did you feel when you got your first cover of *Vogue*?

That was one of the highlights of my life. I think it is every model's dream to be on the cover of *Vogue* magazine. And then having been the first woman of color on the magazine cover doubled the impact for me. And being that it was like a history-making cover—well, it was a very, very special moment in the legacy that continues to this day. For me it was really a pivotal moment in my life—as far as my responsibility as a woman, as a black woman, as a career woman, as a professional, as a black professional in this world and what that stands for, and what women of color look to me for; it really changed my life.

Did you experience these realizations gradually or suddenly, at that moment?

It hit me at that moment. No woman of color had ever been on the cover of *Vogue*—I was appalled by that fact. And before I got the cover, who knew when one ever would be? Along with that came the investigation of who I am, who I am as an African American, and the whole investigation of my history and my roots. It was such a profound

moment for me. So it opened up a whole new avenue of investigation. Who am I? And who I am to the world? What is my purpose in life?

Did that *Vogue* cover change things for models of color?

Yes and no. I love to see the diverse nationalities of women that are represented today in the world of fashion. We live in a world where we can now see that there is beauty in every culture. The mutual respect and understanding of the beauty of every culture just feeds one's own culture, enriches it. It has nothing to do with one being better than the other. Beauty is beauty. So you do see that today, and I think that is due to technology, television—the world is a smaller place. There are still perceptions and ideas of American beauty, standard beauty. America being such a melting pot—they don't really apply. No standard ever did. Still, they try to present it. Then there's the economics. There are the inequalities of the economics which eventually will rectify themselves, but it's taking a long time.

Are there any myths or misconceptions about models that you'd like to address?

There are a lot of myths. But as we really develop ourselves as professionals and as artists, I think that those myths will be dealt with. I think there is the myth of "being thin natu-

rally." The myth of being beautiful—
"I'm really just like anyone else."
That's a myth. There is the myth that
"growing old doesn't bother me."
There is the myth that "I'm as secure
as the next person." I think there are
a lot of myths about the modeling
industry that will be dispelled as we
are more honest about what goes on
in the industry—as we are able to
present the industry so that other
people can really understand it. Otherwise, the myths will continue—that
models are dumb—that models

Photo: Charles Bush/Essence

can't talk and walk at the
same time.

**What advice would you give
to the beginning model?**
I've always encouraged anyone who ever wanted to go
into the profession because it's
been so wonderful for me. It's
actually helped make me who I
am, in a sense. And I know that
if you have the desire to do something—really, really have the
desire—you can accomplish it.
You see it all the time. Someone
might not even be the right height—
but there's always that individual
who comes on the scene and knocks
down all those things that people
said that you had to be, the requirements that you had to have to succeed in that profession. It's always
bending and changing. So anyone

who really wants to do it—I say, that's exactly what they should do. You want to really be in love with what you are doing. You have to be impassioned about it, and then you have to have faith that it is going to happen. So if you have those three things, you're home free!

Tomiko

Tomiko is a promising young model signed to Wilhelmina. We caught up with her between assignments in London.

How were you discovered?
Before Wilhelmina, I was with an extremely small agency, extremely part-time, because I was still going to school, and I would go out on castings once every six months. So I put some pictures together and went in for Wilhelmina's open call, which they have every Tuesday between 10:00 and 10:30. When I went in I was green. I didn't know anything, but they liked what they saw. They saw potential. They actually wanted me to sign that day, which was flooring, because I know that they rarely find anybody at the open call! So that's how it all got started.

Do you have a dream assignment?
Oh, sure—the cover of *Vogue* or

Elle. I worked for *Elle*, which was great. But the cover is something to look forward to.

You are traveling quite a bit. Do you have any travel tips?
Drink a lot of water. Pack light. I overpack; you're only going to need about a quarter of what you pack. Know the currency before you leave. If you don't speak the language, try to brush up on a few phrases—at least "I'm looking for this. I'm lost." Bring traveler's checks and credit cards. I always bring a mug from

Photo: Raven Afandor/Essence

home, a drinking mug. Bring something from home so you feel like you are at home. It helps in London that they do speak English. But I've gone to Italy before, and I didn't really

Photo: Barton Jahncke/Wilhelmina Model Search fashion show

accepting of black models—that they weren't so afraid to use black models. I've been told to my face so many times, "You know, you are a black model, so it's going to be harder for you." I've really become used to hearing that. And it's a shame. I shouldn't be used to hearing that.

Do you think this attitude is changing at all?
I was keeping up with fashion for a couple of years before I started modeling, and it has changed, and it has gotten better—from back in the '70s and '80s—and Beverly Johnson and Naomi Sims, I'm sure they helped, and it's a lot better. But I know what the possibilities are, what they could be, and that's what I'm waiting for.

I think some of the barriers have been broken at this point, but still there are quite a few black models and there are only a few opportunities.
Exactly. Everybody thinks we had Naomi, so we don't need anybody else, but they have a Christy, they have a Linda, a Claudia—they have a variety of top Caucasian models.

Is this attitude as prevalent in London? Is it any different in New York, Paris, Milan?
In the industry it is pretty much the same, and I think it's a little more bla-

enjoy that because I don't speak the language. I'm not looking forward to going to Paris this weekend because I don't speak the language. But I've got my French/English phrase book—it helps to know little phrases here and there. It can be scary. But as long as you have a good agency, and you have people around you that are taking care of you, it can be fine.

What's the downside of modeling?
I wish that people were more

tant here. I just heard this the other day, "Well, you know, you *are* a black model." As far as people and friends and things like that, I haven't seen a problem with it. There is so much race mixing here, it's unbelievable. So I haven't seen it in general, but in the industry, yeah. Milan is worse. I was there for six weeks, and I don't even think I did one magazine. Granted, that was two years ago and I was just getting started. They just said, "Oh, you know, you're too dark, and you're black," and I just had a really bad time—I had a friend who interpreted what they were saying: "Wow, you know these two black girls must be sick, because they are so skinny, you know; all black people are fat." And I'm just looking at them, and you have to laugh. I can't get upset anymore. You just have to laugh.

Who are your favorite photographers, people you'd like to work with?
I don't really have a favorite. I haven't had any bad experiences. I just like working with somebody who's professional and gives me some direction—not too much. I'm one of those models that doesn't need a lot of direction. Tell me what you want and what you are looking for, and I'll try and give that to you, and if I'm not, then you can help me

out a little bit. But just somebody that's fun and not stiff. I've had some opportunities to do some great stuff, and my goal from the start was just to be able to show my grandkids a picture of something that I'd done. But it's turning into a lot more than that, and it's very exciting.

Photo: C. Bruckheimer

10 THE BUSINESS BEHIND THE BUSINESS

Rates of Pay

What do models earn? Generally, a major agency in New York expects its new recruits to earn in excess of $40,000 the first year to warrant continued representation—not bad pay for a seventeen-year-old accustomed to making $6 an hour baby-sitting! If a model is considered editorial, or is unusual looking, an agency may wait things out a little longer, unconcerned that she (or he) is bringing in less revenue than some of the other new faces. They have faith that her time will come and that, when it does, she will more than make up for a sluggish start!

Established models make upwards of $50,000 per year—the average yearly income being $80,000 to $150,000. Top models earn upwards of $200,000 per year. A supermodel's yearly take can be nearly limitless—$500,000 per year to several million. A top male model can earn between $80,000 and $1 million per year, but then, his career can go on for much longer than that of the female model. Male supermodel salaries are on the upswing; some guys are cashing in in the $1 million plus per year range.

The Independent Contractor

Once you have been accepted by an agency, and have booked your first assignment, you are considered an independent contractor. The following are brief descriptions of the paperwork involved in the career of the professional model.

The Agency Contract

An agent who believes in your potential will eventually want you to sign a contract to prevent you

Name _____   Date __/__/__
Address _____   Birthdate __/__/__
                            S S # __-__-__
Phone ( ) _____

AGREEMENT

This letter shall constitute your and my agreement as follows.

1. I hereby engage your services and you accept such engagement to be my sole and exclusive Worldwide Manager for the term of this Agreement in the field of modeling and runway. As such, you shall advise and counsel me in any and all matters regarding publicity and public relations and the general practices of the modeling, entertainment and advertising industries; advise and counsel me regarding the proper formats for presenting myself to third parties, including aspects of makeup, hair, photo composites and formation of a portfolio; and advise and counsel me regarding placements or referrals to secondary agencies in the United States or elsewhere. You shall act as "mother agent" at all times.

2. I hereby appoint you my lawful Attorney-in-Fact and authorize you to collect and receive monies on my behalf, to endorse my name upon and deposit same in your account with any bank, and to retain therefrom all sums due you at any time. I also authorize you to approve and permit the use of my name, photograph, likeness and voice and sign releases on my behalf. This authorization shall include all self promotion for Wilhelmina Models Inc. ie. headsheets, books, electronic media, including but not limited to computer on-line services, the Internet and CD-ROM. This power of attorney is irrevocable during the term of this Agreement and, with respect to any matter for which you are entitled to compensation, thereafter. I hereby assign to you the proceeds of all assignments done by me, against which advance payment has been made by you to me. If, in accordance with your voucher system, you advance me any sums against my fees not yet received and you do not receive collection within six (6) months, I will upon request reimburse you for the sums you advanced to me. Cancellation fees, expenses, foreign billings, advertising agencies and other clients as determined by your accounting office are paid to artist when payment is received by manager. Manager will take all reasonable steps to collect the amounts due with respect thereto. The risk of collection, in connection with artists vouchers, and the legal costs thereto shall be borne entirely by the artist.

3. I agree to seek your counsel in regard to all matters concerning my endeavors in the field of modeling. I shall advise you of all offers of employment submitted to me anywhere in the world with respect to modeling and will refer any inquiries concerning my services to you. I acknowledge that you are not an "artist manager" under the labor code of California or an employment agency in any jurisdiction and you shall not be required or expected to obtain offers of employment for me. It is

also acknowledged that the relationship between me as a model, and you as manager, is one of independent contractor. I warrant that I will be responsible for any government employment tax/insurance/immigration obligations that may be necessary.

4. In consideration of your entering into this agreement and as compensation for the services to be rendered by you hereunder, I agree to pay you an amount equal to twenty (20%) percent of any and all gross monies or other consideration which I receive as a result of agreements (and any renewals or renegotiations thereof) relating to my modeling throughout the world, which agreements are entered into during the term hereof. In addition, I agree to pay you an amount equal to ten(10%) percent of any and all gross monies derived from any television commercials, industrials, usages and or renewal fees as the terms apply to "TV." I agree to pay or reimburse you for all out-of-pocket expenses which you incur from time to time on my behalf.

5. The term of this agreement shall be for a period of five (5) years commencing as of this date, and it will be automatically renewed for five (5) years at a time unless you or I give written notice to the other of the intention to terminate by registered mail at least ninety (90) days prior to the end of the then current term.

6. Any contracts, or work involving future usages, as that term is customarily used, shall be handled by you and you shall receive your compensation in such connection, until the termination of such usages, regardless of the sooner expiration, termination or modification of this agreement.

7. I am aware and agree that you are entitled to receive a service charge from some and/or all of the clients who utilize my services and that you may receive a service charge of fee shall be an additional inducement for you to act on my behalf.

8. This agreement shall be governed by and construed in accordance with the laws of the State of New York applicable to agreements wholly made therein and any dispute arising out of this agreement shall be resolved in the courts of the State and City of New York.

Agreed and Accepted:

WILHELMINA MODELS, INC.

By _____

MODEL   (or parent/guardian)
_____

If any other than Wilhelmina Models, Inc., my parent representative is
_____

My introduction to Wilhelmina Inc. was arranged by
_____

from becoming associated with competing agents. The contract is a simple mutual agreement between the model and the agency, setting the terms by which the model is to be represented. Most agency contracts state that you will accept all modeling assignments through their agency *only*—for the duration of the contract. Agents prefer to manage models on an exclusive basis because they feel more comfortable devoting time and energy to the promotion of a model who has a commitment to them. While agency contracts vary somewhat, the Wilhelmina Models contract can be used as an example.

Wilhelmina Models represents clients under an *exclusive* agreement. This means that, once you are signed to Wilhelmina Models, *only* Wilhelmina Models will manage and guide your modeling career. Agencies in New York and L.A. usually offer exclusive contracts, while agencies in smaller markets may offer agreements that allow a model to freelance with several agencies. The terms of the contract authorize the agency to use the model's name, photograph and likeness, and to sign releases and contracts (power of attorney) on the model's behalf.

Under the Wilhelmina model's contract, the model agrees to pay the agency 20 percent of all gross earnings. This is a standard percentage. The contract is valid for two years, after which it may be renewed. It can, however, be terminated by either the model or the agency with written notice and valid reason for termination.

An agency may choose to end its relationship with a model who continually arrives late for bookings or is generally uncooperative. A model may terminate a contract if she (or he) feels she is not being properly promoted. The following are some additional reasons for a model to consider changing agencies.

- Your agent fails to provide payment for work completed or is constantly making excuses for late payments. You should not have to nag an agent for a promised check.
- Your agent consistently omits booking information or misrepresents assignments. You may want to look for more ethical representation.
- Your agent is disorganized to the point that you end up appearing incompetent to your clients. You may want to look for a more professional agent.

Always have a discussion with your agent before changing agencies, so that he or she is aware of your dissatisfaction and has a chance to correct problems.

The Model Permit

If you are under the age of eighteen, you must obtain a work permit through the board of education in the state in which you plan to work. The permit must be applied for in person. Bring the following documentation:

- a note from your primary care physician, stating that you are in good health
- a copy of your birth certificate
- your social security number

Your agency will inform you of any additional requirements regarding application for this document in your area.

The Voucher

A voucher documents not only a model's rate of pay but also the time she or he arrives at a booking and leaves a booking. These forms are provided by the agency and must be turned in to the agency's accounting department after every booking to ensure that the model's time is properly billed. Be sure to sign your voucher and

AGENCY COPY
(AS ATTORNEY IN FACT FOR)

W₂

WILHELMINA MODELS INC.
(212) 473-0700
300 Park Avenue South
New York, NY 10010
FAX (212) 473-3223

SEND INVOICE TO:

ADDRESS:
CITY   ZIP CODE
STATE
ATTENTION:
SPECIAL BILLING/P.O. #:

MODEL NAME:
DATE OF JOB: USAGE
PRODUCT   STUDIO
RATE   TIME: FROM: TO: $
FITTING FEE   FITTING DATE $
TRAVEL   TIME: $
MISC.
EXPENSES $
AGENCY FEE TO BE ADDED TO THE
TOTAL AMOUNT.   AGENCY FEE $
CHARTER MEMBER OF IMMA
                    TOTAL $

UNIFORM MODEL RELEASE (VALID UPON PAYMENT)

In consideration of receipt of the model fee (inclusive of service fee) as well as any additional usage fees negotiated with my manager, I hereby sell, assign and grant to ____ and ____

Advertising Agency or Publication / Client/Advertiser
the right and permission to copyright and use or publish one (1) photograph or likeness of me in which I may be included in whole or part of composite or reproductions thereof in color or otherwise in the United States for ____ usage: i.e. Print, POS, Pkg, OOH, etc. for ____ months to begin no later than four (4) months later than this date, except that these photos may not be used on TV in any manner. Accordingly, I release and discharge the company and persons named above and persons acting for or on behalf of them from any liability by virtue of any blurring, distortion, alteration, optical illusion, or use in composite form that may occur or be produced in the taking of said pictures or in any processing thereof through completion of the finished product. Note: Products, packaging usage, billboards, point-of-sale, hang tags, exclusivity, endorsements, use of name, TV and any other special usage require separate negotiations. All other releases not valid unless countersigned by model manager. Client's workman's compensation carrier is ____

CLIENT'S SIGNATURE ____   MODEL'S SIGNATURE ____

AGENCY COPY
(AS ATTORNEY IN FACT FOR)

W₂

WILHELMINA MODELS INC.
(212) 473-0700
300 Park Avenue South
New York, NY 10010
FAX (212) 473-3223

SEND INVOICE TO: *B.N. & R. Adv.*

ADDRESS: *550 Madison Ave.*
CITY *NYC*   ZIP CODE *10021*
STATE
ATTENTION: *accounts payable*
SPECIAL BILLING/P.O. #: *PO# 7871450*

MODEL NAME: *Erik Stockholm*
DATE OF JOB: *12/1-10/95*   USAGE *Campaign*
PRODUCT *Monte Fragrance* STUDIO *Studio Y*
RATE *$500 a* TIME: FROM: *9* TO: *5* $*85,000*
FITTING FEE   FITTING DATE
TRAVEL   TIME:
MISC.
EXPENSES
AGENCY FEE TO BE ADDED TO THE
TOTAL AMOUNT.   AGENCY FEE $
CHARTER MEMBER OF IMMA
                    TOTAL $*85,000*

UNIFORM MODEL RELEASE (VALID UPON PAYMENT)

In consideration of receipt of the model fee (inclusive of service fee) as well as any additional usage fees negotiated with my manager, I hereby sell, assign and grant to ____ and ____

Advertising Agency or Publication / Client/Advertiser
the right and permission to copyright and use or publish *all uses type makes* ____ usage: i.e. Print, POS, Pkg, OOH, etc. for ____ months to begin no later than four (4) months later than this date, except that these photos may not be used on TV in any manner. Accordingly, I release and discharge the company and persons named above and persons acting for or on behalf of them from any liability by virtue of any blurring, distortion, alteration, optical illusion, or use in composite form that may occur or be produced in the taking of said pictures or in any processing thereof through completion of the finished product. Note: Products, packaging usage, billboards, point-of-sale, hang tags, exclusivity, endorsements, use of name, TV and any other special usage require separate negotiations. All other releases not valid unless countersigned by model manager. Client's workman's compensation carrier is ____

CLIENT'S SIGNATURE ____   MODEL'S SIGNATURE ____

have the client or photographer sign on the lines provided before leaving a booking. Most major agencies advance payment to their models on a biweekly basis. This practice is based on the **voucher system.** Models signed to smaller agencies may not be paid until after the agency has actually received payment from the client.

The Model Release

Your agency voucher acts as a limited model release. The agency will inform you of any restrictions that you should itemize on the release for a particular booking. Do not sign any other releases at a booking unless the agency has informed you of this additional document prior to the booking. A model release is a legal document that dictates usage rights and payment for your image. If you sign it, you may be waiving your right to future payments (for usage rights) that are your due.

If you are asked to sign something other than a voucher on a shoot, respond politely but firmly: "I'd be happy to cooperate. Let me take this back to the agency. They will complete it and have it returned to you." If you are pressured further, telephone the agency and ask your booker for instructions.

Taxes

Once you are earning a steady income as a model, it is wise to invest in a tax accountant familiar with the entertainment industry, to prepare your quarterly filing correctly. Be sure to carefully save and file the receipts for these services as well as receipts for all other work-related expenses. Make a note on the back of each and every receipt—the five *W*'s: Who, What, Where, When and Why.

All of the following can be deducted as expenses relating to your business:

Printing of composite cards
Postage for mailings
Testing fees
Answering machine
Photographs and printing
Portfolio
Clothing and accessories used
    specifically for modeling
    assignments
Haircuts, manicures
Promotional materials (i.e., the fee
    for including your photo in the
    agency promotional book)
Accounting and tax preparation fees
Acting classes and coaching, voice,
    singing and dance classes
Telephone
Office supplies
Auto expenses
Business meals and entertainment
Business gifts
Union dues (Screen Actors Guild,
    AFTRA and Actors Equity)
Travel expenses, including out-of-
    town car rentals, airline tickets,
    buses, taxis, trains, meals and
    lodgings

The Paycheck

The paycheck you receive from your agency will list gross earnings and deductions. The agency's commission (usually 20 percent) will be deducted from the total, along with any advance payments the agency has made on your behalf. Advance payments may include cash advances, messenger services, head sheet and promotional book fees, postage and overnight shipping charges.

11 THE PEOPLE WHO MAKE IT ALL HAPPEN

First there's you. You make it happen. You build a portfolio, meet photographers, designers and clients. The right agent shapes and guides your career. A prominent photographer uses you in an editorial story. You model the clothing of a famous designer on a runway in Paris. Another designer sees the show and books you for his or her print campaign—your career gathers momentum. You study the business, maintain an attitude of professionalism. An editor of a fashion magazine thinks you're right for the cover of the magazine. The photographer agrees. You are on your way!

Let's take a closer look at some of the industry professionals who will help you achieve your goals.

him (or her), who understands his vision and can use her face and body to make it clear and tangible for the camera—will hire that model over and over again. It has always been this way. Irving Penn had Lisa Fonssagrives, Richard Avedon had Suzy Parker, Helmet Newton has always had his favorite models. Of course, if a photographer is as powerful as these (today we have Steven Meisel, Patrick Demarchalier, Bruce Weber in similar positions) this sort of matchmaking can do wonders for a model's career. Steven Meisel was responsible for promoting the famous (and infamous) "trinity"—Christy Turlington, Linda Evangelista and Naomi Campbell—by photographing them together over and over in luscious editorial sto-

The Photographer

The model-photographer relationship is a very special one. When a photographer finds that he has a certain rapport with a particular model the results on film can be magical. A photographer who finds his *muse*—a model who inspires

ries. These girls were already successful, but the extra focus from a photographer like Meisel gave even more momentum to their careers.

In conjunction with magazine fashion editors, a photographer will sometimes help create a model's unique "look." If Steven Meisel is shooting an up-and-coming model for the cover of *Italian Vogue*, he, the editors, the stylist, hair and makeup people will meet to discuss the look they want to achieve. This may mean an entire day of grooming the model prior to the actual

Photo: Lynn Ban

shoot—cutting and coloring her hair, experimenting with makeup to find what best suits her features—a total makeover.

Kevin Jones explains just how powerful the endorsement of a photographer can be: "Designers want to have images, they want to have faces. They want stars. Stars bring

in the media attention, produce great campaigns. A designer will turn to a photographer and say, 'Who are you using right now? Who's hot? I want her in my show. I want him in my print campaign.'"

Doug Ordway has photographed supermodels Amber Valletta, Nadege, Nadja Auermann and Kristen McMenamy for a variety of clients ranging from magazines like *German Vogue* to designers like Gianni Versace. He credits photographer Bruce Weber, whom he assisted, as the greatest influence in his career. Bruce, he says, "really educated me as far as style and fashion editorial is concerned." Doug comments on the industry from the photographer's perspective.

What kind of rapport between the model and the photographer do you think is necessary on an editorial shoot?

Rapport is so important that I do not like to book models without meeting them first. The personality is a major part to me. My favorite way to shoot is where I give the model a concept. And I'll say, "Play up on this concept. Work with it." So I need a model who understands what I'm aiming for. I need a model with range—who can be an actress. You do need to show clothes, but you need to pull this look out of the eyes. You make her feel that she is the sexiest, most beautiful woman alive. And the way that she stands there, the way she carries herself, the body language, is all going to be incorporated through that.

It's a matter of confidence, and it's a matter of a psychological connection, but it depends on the clothes and the image you're trying to project, and it depends on the girl—if she can come up with that.

What skills can a model develop so that she/he knows what a photographer is talking about when a certain idea is presented?

I think it's having very broad horizons, you know. There are a lot of beautiful girls out there, but there is a lot of knowledge that is also needed to be a model. It's not that you can just be beautiful—stand there and look beautiful. That gets boring, real quick. If I give the direction "I want you to be like Sophia Loren in Vittorio de Sica's *Yesterday, Today, and Tomorrow,*" you know that film, and you can say, "Okay, let me think, Sophia Loren was very sexy," you know what she looked like, and you can incorporate that vision. It's especially important with the big photographers, the big magazines; they always want you to be an actress. And if you know all those old actresses in all the films in the past, then you can really know what is going on in the shooting, otherwise you are in the dark.

If you have a go-see and a number of models walk into the room, what do you look for? I know it will be different things for different types of shoots, but can you generalize?

I look for a girl who is comfortable with herself, who projects the image: "Hey, here I am, use me. I'm right for this job."

Is there a difference, generally, between the catalog model and the editorial model?

There's a big difference. The catalog model can simply stand there on the set with a pleasant attitude—the shots are dictated—there doesn't have to be as much of the actress mentality. An editorial model has to give more of herself and be more creative.

By what criteria are models hired?

The magazines, advertisers and various catalogs prefer certain looks—certain types of girls that they want to use. More specifically, in casting editorial stories, certain girls fit the look of certain stories too, so of course they are going to consider that. Usually there is some concern for the photographer's choice. The photographer should be happy with the person that he is shooting, otherwise he will not be inspired to do his best work. If you like the look of the girl or the guy that you are shooting, you have much more passion in doing it. If you don't, you can't pull that passion out. When we are considering models, I will throw out a name and say, "Okay, I want this girl." They'll say, "No, we don't like her, but what about this one?" I'll say, "No." So you go back and forth till somehow it comes to a point where you're both happy with the girl that you've chosen.

What goes into the planning of an editorial shoot?

Plans are made following the fashion shows, after all the collections are seen . . . Milan, Paris, New York, a little bit of London, a little bit of Spain. The fashion director or the creative director will come up with an idea which she feels is geared to the season. They'll decide which photographer can deliver the images they've envisioned and what kind of models will best suit that image. Along with the photographer, they choose appropriate hair and makeup people and models. It all depends on what they want to project. If the image is very distinct, like "mod" or "waif," we sometimes get models who are a flash in the pan—they are only really suited for that one look, that one season. Kate Moss was able to transcend the waif look because she's grown up some. She's become more of a woman, and she's transcended that whole thing. But some of the other girls who were popular as waifs have disappeared. So a girl can be right for a

look for that season and then find out one or two seasons down the road that she is not doing anything. And usually the models who are right just for a season are not able to transfer into advertising and catalog work, because catalog work represents your classic sense of what is pretty in America. Then there are girls like Christy Turlington or Linda Evangelista whose looks transcend anything. They have commercial appeal and they can do something extremely editorial. They possess both sensibilities. That's why they're so successful for so long.

Who are your favorite models?

Christy Turlington . . . mostly because of her natural beauty and her mentality. Also, Kristen McMenamy—the personality again—is wonderful. She's a fun person. She's great to work with. She cares about the work. I've had days where I've had to do forty photographs with her, which is unreal. Once I even had food poisoning, so I was throwing up between shots. But if I didn't have Kristen as a model, I wouldn't have been able to do it. That day, I basically set up my lights—nice, clean, pretty soft light; they wanted something that was a little more commercial—and put her up there. She would go into a pose instantly. She almost contorts herself. She does this thing where she lets her shoulders go and she feels the shape of the clothes and the way they should look. And she looks at herself in the mirror before she gets on the set to know how the shape should look, which angle will make the dress shine, which angle her hair looks best . . . She'll get up there. She'll do the posing—knows what it is going to be already. I would come back from the bathroom, and she would play the role. We'd get the shot right away—and I'd run back to the bathroom and pass out. Many of the other big girls couldn't do it. They would complain. Kristen will go down as one of the best professional models because of her attitude and her extraordinary ability to show clothes.

That brings us to the question of attitude. What should a model's attitude be?

It's got to be difficult when you're being told day after day, moment after moment, how gorgeous and beautiful you are. It's bound to go to anyone's head. And it's the girls—like I use Christy Turlington as the main example—who have not let it get to their head. They are beautiful people inside. Helena Christensen is another good example. She'll be working on location somewhere, say they're in India shooting, and she'll spend two extra days walking around with her camera, taking beautiful photographs of the Indian children. She gives so much to these

photographs. I think that it is important to have something besides just the modeling. If you're constantly being pampered, putting on beautiful clothing, and being told, "You're gorgeous. You're beautiful. You're wonderful," it becomes hard to maintain a balance. If you have something to take you away from that—like what Helena does when she goes out and takes pictures of these little kids . . . wearing tattered clothing, who may not have enough to eat, and she brings out the beauty in these kids, that kind of brings her head back down to earth. Kristen McMenamy has a baby that she loves very much, and that keeps her centered.

What advice would you give a model just starting out?

I think sometimes the newer girls get distracted and disappointed because they're not a hit right away. But it's almost better not to be. If you are going to be around for a while, it takes a little while to get there. If you don't make it right away, it doesn't mean you're not going to. So my advice is, be patient. Have confidence in yourself. Have a knowledge of the business. You have to decide whose opinion you respect—which agents, photographers, designers, hair and makeup people. A lot of people are going to tell you you should cut your hair, you should dye your hair, you should dye

Photo: Doug Ordway/AMICA

A sinistra, body in tulle stretch ricamato con paillettes e
pantaloni in voile aperti su un lato, firmati *Ritmo di Perla*
come, qui accanto, l'abito con paillettes

it black, you should lose weight, you
should gain weight. You have
to take all that in and decide
what is right for you and whose
opinion you respect.

I think it is good for a girl,
especially when she is new and
looking to have pictures and stuff
like that, to hook up with a photographer who really appreciates
her look, who will help her
broaden her look. Even if it is a test
photographer, if you respect what
he does, you respect his taste, a

Photo: Doug Ordway/AMICA

photographer can guide a new model. Of course, people like Steven [Meisel] do this very well. They take a girl in—I know, because I assisted him at one time—and spend a full day recreating the girl, cutting the hair, dying the brows, recutting the hair, coloring, then recoloring—until it's just right. If you can find someone who you respect enough to let do that, that's big for a girl. Someone with Steven's power can really get a model started. Take the shows last season—the girls were like these new Steven Meisel girls, ugly, drugged-out looking, in a way, a little bit dirty looking. That was the look that they wanted. And if Steven decides he wants to create a new bunch—say squeaky clean girl-next-door types—well, then they'll be all over the runways.

If there were one thing about the industry that you could change, what would it be?

The mentality. The mentality of being better than other people. Just try to have fun and do our jobs and make some great pictures. Too often, egos get involved—on shoots someone always tries to be the most important, and that's the mentality that I don't like. It should be a real group effort. The model shouldn't try to be more important than the hair and makeup people, and so on. It's a group effort. Let's all work together and have fun with it!

The Photographer's Top Ten Pet Peeves

Here's a collection of complaints gathered from some of New York's finest.

1. The model who shows up for a booking looking altogether different from the composite card or portfolio from which she was booked. Her hair has been cut short or is a different color. Her measurements are incorrect. She's gained ten pounds. Now the clothes don't fit.
2. The model who chews gum on the set.
3. The model who (for various reasons) can't stay awake on the set or can't keep still for the photograph. One photographer explained that, because of the lighting requirements for a certain client, he had to shoot at a relatively long exposure (¼ second). The model was "vibrating so hard" that her image on the processed film was blurred with motion. The entire job had to be reshot with a different girl.
4. The model who turns up for a booking with family members, friends or small dogs in tow. (The exception, of course, is the very young model who is expected to bring a parent along.)
5. The model who cannot get off the phone to get the shot.
6. The model who wears her Walkman on the set.
7. The model who plays Nintendo on the set.
8. The model who delays the shoot by arriving late and then charges overtime.
9. The model with an attitude of superiority, who treats the crew poorly.
10. Various types of unprofessional behavior: discussing fees with the client or other models, talking behind the backs of other models and members of the crew and generally failing to cooperate with everyone to get the job done.

The Fashion Editor/Stylist

The fashion editor or stylist provides editorial direction, a sense of a story line. She or he will dress the model in an interesting way, paying attention to the details, choosing shoes, hosiery and accessories. In a magazine situation there is a whole army of assistants who actually go out and get the clothing from various designers and assemble it for the fashion editor to review. The fashion editor or editor in chief approves each ensemble before it goes into the magazine.

Stylists and fashion editors are responsible for securing the best of the collections each season for their respective editorial shoots. The best attracts the best. Top photographers, magazines and editors get first pick of the collection clothing, practically right off the catwalks. Some of the bigger fashion magazines are notorious for holding on to the best clothing for weeks, even months at a time. Thus, a sort of editorial monopoly is created. If competing magazines hope to meet their deadlines they must make do with their second choices.

A tremendous selection of clothing, shoes and accessories is gathered for an editorial shoot. Most of these items will never be photographed. The fashion editor and stylist put together the most enticing looks for each photograph; the outfits that most fit the theme of the story. They fit and dress the models, style the clothing so that it looks alluring in every shot. Then they make notes—clothing descriptions, color, fabric content, cut and style—for the writer who will generate copy to accompany the photographs.

On an advertising shoot, a freelance stylist is hired to gather the appropriate garments for the models and talent, fit and coordinate the outfits and make sure they look good for the shot. If the clothing is to be the feature of the advertisement, as in a fashion campaign, the designer and his or her assistants will choose the garments, fit and style them.

The stylist's best friend is a model who fits the clothing and knows how to move so that the clothing always looks great. Study the garment you are about to model for the camera. Turn this way and that. See how it falls best. Note what is striking or interesting about the garment and show it off. Study the magazines. Use your favorite model as an example. Don't mimic her, but do learn from her and from other successful models. Then develop your own sense of the clothing, your own unique style of movement.

The Art Director

Some art directors are very hands-on. They are on the set, adding something to a photographer's vision, but this is rare. Usually an art director chooses a photographer and crew he (or she) knows will execute the task faithfully. He then receives the film once it has been edited, works with the photographer on the images that have been chosen, then lays out and puts type on a page. In advertising and catalog projects, an art director may be present to see that the shots are executed correctly so as to fit with type and graphics.

The Designer

Certain designers are famous for their ability to create an image—to pluck a young girl (or guy) from anonymity and plaster her all over the world's catwalks and fashion magazines. Calvin Klein has done it time and time again. Kate Moss is a good example. One season, Calvin needed a model that he could pile clothes on for a layered effect—a smaller model—Kate was it. Kate was perfect for Calvin.

Certain designers need certain kinds of models. Part of the beginning model's job is to make herself aware of the designers advertising in the magazines. What type of model is Giorgio Armani using, and why? Where do I fit in? Versace needs models with long limbs and curves to show off his body-conscious designs. Am I right for his campaign? Geoffrey Beene needs a smaller-boned, more delicate model with classic features. Will I enhance the image he is creating? Study the magazines, the designers, their work, the ad campaigns they run. Discuss your findings with your agent so that the two of you can explore additional ways of promoting you as a model.

The Hairstylist

There are very few top models whose hair Garren of Garren, at Henri Bendel, *has not cut!* Some of his regular clients include Linda Evangelista, Amber Valletta, Naomi Campbell, Trish Goff, Christy Turlington, Shalom Harlow, Kristen McMenamy and Michelle Hicks. Garren is also responsible for Madonna's platinum waves and Isabella Rossellini's signature geometric cut.

The secret of beautiful hair, insists Garren, is good health overall: "Maintaining a healthy diet and drinking ample amounts of water benefit the hair." He adds, "One should select a gentle cleansing shampoo and alternate it with a deep cleansing one. Conditioning after every shampooing is essential. Hair should also be deep conditioned once weekly. Good, frequent haircuts will keep hair at its best."

A model just starting out should, according to Garren, "wait [before making major changes] until she has her first big break with a noted photographer or fashion magazine. This business is about creating. Those involved want something they can shape and mold. Timing is so essential in a model's career. A model will be specifically groomed for a special assignment, like the cover of *Vogue:* At this time it is up to the hairstylist to find the balance between the photographer's vision and the maximum potential of the model. You are creating a look as well as a fantasy and must be prepared for almost anything. At the same time, a girl will have to live and work with this cut for a while. Her career will be affected by it and by the visions of the individuals who help create her look. When I consider a cut for a particular girl, I examine facial bone structure, body proportion and body language— the way a girl moves and holds herself. I also must consider her personality. A great deal of thought goes into this, not only on my part, but on the part of the photographer and the makeup artist. Of course, lighting and makeup can be changed almost instantly. Hair takes its time to grow—the cut must deliver."

"An established model," notes Garren, "can give her career new life by making a change—a different cut or color. Once again, timing is essential. You must know what to do, when to do it and what kind of statement to make. In the end, I follow my instincts. Being that I am so involved with the industry—with years of experience—the models trust me to create something that they will be happy with and which will only serve to advance their careers."

The Makeup Artist

On the set of a photo shoot, it is up to the makeup artist to translate the photographer's (or fashion editor's) vision of the model into a tangible representation in keeping with the theme of the overall story. Makeup artist Laura Mercier has created natural glowing looks for many of the world's leading actresses. Among them are Catherine Deneuve, Isabelle Adjani, Meryl Streep, Glenn Close, Isabella Rossellini and Lauren Hutton. Laura is also a favorite of Elizabeth Arden model Vendela. Here, Laura describes her holistic approach to makeup and skin care.

What are the responsibilities of the makeup artist on the set of a photo shoot?

I always try to facilitate a clear understanding and a good connection between the photographer, the model and the makeup artist as far as makeup is concerned. It's important to make concrete the ideas of the photographer. Sometimes the photographer can not express himself in the matter of makeup, so we have to translate his ideas into something technical about the makeup—at the same time working with the kind of face we have—the model booked for the assignment. Of course, the lighting must be considered, along with the concept of the entire shoot.

It's also about the translation of the face of the model, to make it as beautiful as is possible, not turn off her beauty—you know what I mean, by putting on too much. Or by doing something which is not conducive to the theme of the shooting.

How do you decide which features to accentuate on a face?

By observing, by emphasizing what has to be emphasized according to the light, according to the theme of the shooting. If we have to do something really glamorous and sexy, I'm going to emphasize the sexy side of the face. On the contrary, for something very natural and very young, I'm going to emphasize whatever can be translated in a natural way. So I'm going to observe what can be emphasized and choose some elements. I am going to emphasize the eyes or the mouth, according to what the face gives. If the face has beautiful, beautiful eyes, if the mouth is a little bit less powerful; then maybe we can really go for the eyes.

How should a model care for her skin?

The model should *care,* that's for sure. We try to give some advice without sounding too parental. Many young girls just want to have fun, and they don't feel they need to worry about their skin. But it's very important, first of all, that they protect their skin in the sun—and to react against stupid people who tell them to get a dark tan in two days. That can destroy the skin for a long time, unfortunately, even at a young age. These responsibilities should be taken on early. It's a part of the job. It's a part of the job to take care of themselves.

What about moisturizing?

Yes, moisturizing, but not overmoisturizing—meaning a model should really use something that is right for her age and type of skin. Some have a tendency to think that because they have makeup on all day, are stressed out because of the long hours, they should choose something that is very rich. This is a mistake, because after a while the skin begins to adapt and need something richer. Instead of taking something too rich for your skin, think about not going to a party. Get some sleep, or take a day off if you are feeling stressed. That's part of taking care of the skin as well.

And cleansing?

Makeup should be removed thoroughly as soon as the shoot is finished. You must really, really pay attention. Invest in a good cleansing product and make sure you remove every bit of makeup—everything— otherwise there's a tendency to break out. And then, as a model, you are in trouble.

And if the skin does break out, what do you recommend?

See a good dermatologist immediately. A dermatologist will give you a schedule to follow as far as cleansing and moisturizing are concerned. He will also give advice regarding diet, alcohol, smoking. Sometimes prescriptions for antibiotics are given if the condition is serious.

Remember that the skin is a reflection of what is happening inside the body. So if you stress out, this direct connection with the nerves will affect your complexion. If you are depressed, it shows too. It's a matter of degree and varies from person to person. It doesn't happen to everyone right away either. Some girls are partying and smoking and drinking and taking drugs, and they have perfect skin. They have perfect skin for a while. It hits a few years later. And that's why even if I sound like a grandma, I try to be open about it. But you obviously can't tell a girl who is on drugs, "Stop drugs!" You can mention a little something if they are open to it at one point in the conversation, just to make sure that they know and they make the choice. I try to bring it up whenever I can and it's appropriate, otherwise there is nothing you can do. Cigarettes are the worst enemies—cigarettes and the sun.

What does cigarette smoking do to the skin?

It makes the skin turn gray and green and lose its glow. It thickens the skin as well, and ages the skin prematurely.

Models are constantly traveling. Do you have any tips to prevent skin from drying out?

Most models do not wear makeup when they travel, which is good. Clean the skin often during the flight. Put a nice moisturizer on for an overnight flight. When you wake up, spray with some floral water, and moisturize again, over it. I recommend that you have little samples of cleanser and a good moisturizer and a spray of rose water or floral water. Try to sleep on the plane, especially if you must work the morning you arrive. Drink mineral water without bubbles. Try to avoid the airplane food as well, because, unfortunately, that makes you tired and it makes you swollen. Another good trick is to drink hot water with lemon all the time. You'll go to the bathroom often, of course, because it is very diuretic. Eat a healthy meal before you get on the plane, and do not eat anything on the plane.

How do you feel about cosmetic surgery for models?

I tend to be against it for models. If you are a model, you are far from ugly—nothing is too horribly wrong. Don't change your face or body. It's a part of your personality. It is a very European way to think. I'm afraid, although I love America and will be adopting a lot of things in America, I still fight against that because it kills the personality. I'm against models who redo their noses systematically. Some of them have done a little something somewhere and it worked, but it's very rare.

Then there is the rush to get the lips pumped up to be more full. [Altering] lips is even worse, because in the morphology of the face everything is combined so it goes together. So if you have the face of a model, meaning if you are pretty enough or interesting enough to be in this business, everything is part of your unique personality. Nobody is perfect, not even the top girls. So you correct a little something with makeup. You correct it with light. But if you correct it with surgery, then it's definitive. It's not fun anymore because it is not part of the personality. Part of the personality has been lost forever.

Imagine if Linda [Evangelista] was pumping her lips with silicone, because they are a little bit smaller than some other model's. Can you imagine? She would be completely different. She's not Linda Evangelista anymore.

Fortunately the idea of beauty is changing for the good. Now we can pay attention to the personality—to beauty in all its various forms. So we even show models with bags under the eyes, with practically no makeup, just the way they are. Some women out there find this depressing. It might not be the standard of attractiveness, but at least we are more open to looking at a human being instead of looking at everything superficially. So it's okay to show someone who is not completely perfect but has a glow of fantastic beauty, or a very interesting personality. And this personality will show the clothes as well, if not better than, the image of someone completely and artificially constructed.

12 Tips for the Model Body

Health

Your health affects your looks, your energy—everything you do as a model. Maintaining it must be your primary concern and part of your professional routine. You will book more work if you consistently get sufficient sleep, eat a balanced diet and maintain an exercise routine. Modeling will wear you out very quickly if you are not in the best of health. You'll soon learn to guard your health carefully—even selfishly.

Skin Care

If you are healthy, your skin will reflect it. Diet, rest and exercise are basic to a smooth, glowing complexion. After that, skin-care routines are as varied as are models themselves. Supermodel Beverly Johnson recommends meditation, herbalism and aroma therapy. These, she feels, are powerful beautifiers because they affect the way we feel—our sense of well-being—and that inner beauty can't help but be reflected in our appearance. Another model, with skin that is sensitive to many products, swears by the use of a mild makeup remover, followed by a splashing rinse with tap water.

Model Hair

A working model's hair is usually washed daily to rid it of the products that are used for a typical photo shoot. All that shampooing, blow-drying, curling, crimping, gels, hair spray can take a toll. More and more hairstylists, sympathetic to the model's need to keep her hair in top condition, are using gentler products—natural nondrying pomades and sprays, molecular (steam) curlers, spray conditioners and moisturizers. But a model's hair still needs a little extra special treatment from its owner.

Hair Care Tips

1. **Condition with heat.** When you condition your hair, add a little heat—from a helmet hair dryer or even a blow dryer. Work the con-

ditioner through your hair. Cover
hair in a plastic shower cap and
apply heat. Heat opens up the
cuticle, allowing the conditioner
to penetrate the shaft of the hair.
Let the conditioner soak in for at
least ten minutes. Then rinse it out
thoroughly, gradually finishing
the rinse with cool water. The
cool water closes the cuticle so
hair is protected from the elements.

2. **Trim your hair often.** Trim your
hair every six weeks to prevent
breakage and split ends, which
can travel up the hair, thinning
the strands and weakening the
hair overall.

3. **Comb wet hair gently.** Hair is
fragile when wet, so treat it gently, combing it with a wide-tooth
comb. Never brush it. As hair
dries, it shrinks, so never tie it
back tightly while it is wet as this
will cause breakage.

4. **Garren's guidelines for the
black model's hair:** If you have
very curly or frizzy hair, you can
relax it. This makes it smooth and
allows for more options and a
greater variety of looks. Hair
weaving and extensions offer
even more alternatives. Of
course, you should always have
a reliable professional who is
experienced with ethnic hair handle your hair.

The Model Diet

First, try not to make a
habit of switching from
diet to diet. Simple
healthful foods will give
you the energy an active model
needs. Just what Mama said—three
balanced meals a day, and you can't
go wrong. Plenty of fresh vegetables
and fruit will keep your skin looking its best. Limit sugary and fried
foods to a special treat once a week.
Combined with exercise, such a diet
will allow you to maintain your
ideal weight within a pound or two.

It is just as important to eat
enough of the right foods as it is not
to overindulge in the wrong ones.
Eating disorders, including periods
of self-inflicted starvation
(anorexia nervosa), and periods of
bingeing followed by purging
(bulimia), can plague the model
who becomes obsessed with weight
and dieting. A model suffering from
these afflictions will find her health
and career slipping away in short
order. *Models who are too thin do*

not work! More importantly, without timely treatment, these disorders can result in death.

Several warning signs predict the onset of illness: extended periods of dieting (fad dieting), misuse of diuretics or laxatives, excessive exercise, depression, weight loss without dieting, use of diet (speed) pills.

If you notice that you are developing any of these behaviors or symptoms, don't be afraid to talk to your agent, your physician and a psychologist. They are familiar with these disorders, understand their severity and will get you the help you need before it's too late. And believe me, they've seen and heard it all before. Eating disorders are not news in the modeling industry. You will not be ridiculed. You will be taken seriously and you will be put in touch with professionals who will introduce you to ways of coping with stress—balancing diet, work, rest and exercise.

Dieting Tips

1. Whatever is in the fridge, *you will eat!* So shop when you are not too hungry and stock up on healthful foods.
2. Allow yourself unlimited snacks! Choose from the following favorites: sweet baby carrots, celery hearts, steamed artichokes with lemon and mustard, air-popped popcorn, apples and fresh fruit salad.
3. Keep plenty of herb teas handy: Mint tea is especially refreshing. Berry teas (especially those with black cherry) have some natural sweetness without the sugar or the calories of juices. Chamomile tea is relaxing at bedtime and warms you up without caloric intake (calories also produce heat).
4. Bring a sweater! If you are unsure of the conditions under which you'll be working, be sure to bring extra clothing to keep warm. Some people's appetites go up when the temperature drops. They are craving heat from the calories food provides.

Exercise

A healthy body is fit, toned and curvy. It's muscles that create curves, not bulging muscles, but long, toned muscles. No matter how much attention you pay to your diet, you will not look your best or feel your best until you find an exercise routine that is comfortable for you. It may mean working out with a personal trainer at home or at a gym. Or dance classes, swimming, or in-line skating may be more to your liking. An aerobic workout three times a week that emphasizes cardiovascular fitness and muscle toning (not bulking up) is ideal for female as well as male models.

Makeup

As a model, you will, in time, learn all the secrets from the professional makeup artists with whom you work. Until then you need be aware only of the basics. Keep your skin clean and moisturized and wear as little makeup as possible to go-sees and appointments. Excessive makeup clogs pores, causes breakouts and even allergic reactions. A light sunscreen is a good idea. Think along the lines of protecting and maintaining your skin rather than camouflaging it under bases and powders. If you really can't leave the house without a little bit of enhancement, keep it to a minimum. A dab of conditioning gloss on your lips and a coat of dark brown mascara on your lashes should suffice.

You may be accustomed to seeing your face in the mirror with lots of color—blush and eye shadow, bright lips. Save it for evening. I can't tell you how many beginning models we've had to drag off to the sink to have their faces wiped free of gummy coverings. Photographers and clients want to see a "blank canvas," a clean, clear complexion and a young-looking face. That's why you have a portfolio—to show what you look like made up to varying degrees. In time, you'll get used to the fresh-faced new you.

Cosmetic Surgery

Cosmetic surgery is a very serious step, and one that we do not encourage, especially for teenage models just starting out. Young people experiencing various degrees of uncertainty over an emerging self-image are prone to consider plastic surgery a quick fix for their problems. Disappointment can become depression when a teenager finds that, not only is she less than thrilled with the results of a costly, painful procedure, but her problems are still the same. Remember that plastic surgery is not something that will guarantee your success as a model. Even the most perfect features cannot guarantee that success. In fact, an unusual characteristic may prove to be an advantage, enabling you to stand out from thousands of other models. Think of Cindy Crawford's trademark mole (which she was advised to have removed), or Linda Evangelista's upturned nose. More and more, models are showing off distinguishing attributes—idiosyncracies that make them outstanding—rather than adapting to some preconceived notion of beauty.

If you must entertain the thought of cosmetic surgery, at least wait until you are finished growing. Your body is still changing during the teenage years, and it is difficult for a plastic surgeon, no matter how accomplished, to accurately forecast the results of a procedure until after the body has grown to full height and proportion. Even your face is changing. The cheekbones

that you can barely discern under their layer of eighteen-year-old puppy fat may (having nothing to do with diet) emerge dramatically at twenty-one.

If you insist upon considering cosmetic surgery, be thorough in your study of the procedure you have chosen. Don't be afraid or embarrassed to ask questions. Be sure that your surgeon is certified by the American Board of Plastic Surgery. Ask to see before and after photographs of the surgeon's work. Ask how many of that type of procedure the surgeon has performed—how many he or she currently performs per month? Find out about the risks involved—*all the risks*, including those generated by general anesthesia. In short, be an informed consumer. And don't expect your life to change dramatically or your career to suddenly take off as a result of an alteration of your face or figure.

13 THE LIFESTYLE OF THE MODEL

Rebecca Gayheart is a model and actress with Wilhelmina Models who has enjoyed remarkable success as the "Noxzema Girl," as a cover girl for magazines such as *Sassy* and *New Woman* and as an emerging starlet. Past credits include a starring role in the television series *Loving*, and the popular series *Beverly Hills, 90210*. Here, she talks with us about lifestyle, hopes and dreams for the future, and the importance of attitude, professionalism and perseverance.

Photo: Troy House/*Tell* magazine

Rebecca, how did you get started?
I was in Kentucky, with a small agency in my hometown. They sent me to New York. I was with Elite first—then I met Natasha at Wilhelmina, and I switched and went with her.

You've also been doing a lot of acting. Is that where you are headed?
Acting is what I've always wanted to do. Modeling just sort of happened and became a stepping-stone. I got a little sidetracked with modeling. But after I came back from Europe I went to Strasberg's [Actors'] Studio, where I studied for two years. Then I went out and got an acting agent, and since then I've been focusing more on acting, although I haven't completely stopped modeling.

What was it like, modeling in Europe?
I went to Milan, and work was okay. For me, modeling was strange. I'm 5'7", so for modeling I'm very short. I always did pretty well, but I never really did break the high-fashion end of it.

How did you feel when you got the Noxzema campaign?
I was just happy to have booked a job, basically. I didn't realize it was going to turn out to be what it turned out to be. I didn't know how visible it was going to make me. I did the commercials first, and then they called and we did print ads and more commercials. So it was good. And actually Noxzema played a part in getting my acting agent. Agents had seen me on the commercials, and they were sort of crawling

around looking for me. And about the same time I had just had a meeting with a manager, an agent from William Morris called up looking for me. So it all sort of ties in, everything complements everything else.

Photo: Troy House/Tell magazine

What's your advice to the beginning model?

Well, I would say that, if it's your passion, if it's something you really want to do, go for it. Don't spend a lot of money on it. I don't believe in "professional photos" in small towns. I think that is sort of a scam. So get your brother to take some snapshots.

Are there any misconceptions about modeling that you'd like to address?

Well, it's just not as glamorous as people think it is. I'm from a small town in Kentucky, and I'd only been in New York for about a month and a half, and I was happy to be doing small catalog bookings. And people were like "How come you're not doing *Vogue*?" It's a little more complicated than that. It's a lot of hard work, and I think that people sometimes forget that models do work hard. Then too, it can also be a very lonely business. You're traveling by yourself all the time. You're always making friends and then leaving them, dropping them again. There are a lot of aspects to it that make you a really strong person, though. I think models, if they are level headed, come out of the business stronger people—very well rounded, actually.

What is the best thing about modeling?
Well, of course, the money. That was my big incentive. And also traveling. You know, there is no other job in which at fifteen, you get to go, to Japan and Milan and Germany.

Tell us about your experience in Japan.
Usually you negotiate a contract with an agency in Japan before you leave to go there. So everything is all set up. You have someone picking you up at the airport, taking you to your apartment, and giving you maps for your first job. And it's quite nice. They really take care of you there. It's not like in Milan, where you're just sort of thrown into this crazy city. Most of the girls are really young when they go to Japan. That's another reason why they are so well looked after. . . . I was doing Homebound [work/study program] because I was still in high school when I was there, so I had to do my homework and things, and they would actually take me to a Japanese school so that I could take my exams. That's how strict they were.

How do you feel about education for models?
Oh, definitely finish high school! Being a high school dropout is sort of looked down on, so just for your own ego and your own pride, finish high school at least. As for university—I think models can do that later. This is a young business, and I believe in taking advantage of the opportunities in front of you. But I think models should always make plans for the future, because it's not a career that's going to be around forever.

If you can succeed in the modeling business, you can leave the modeling business and open up a restaurant, or have your own line of clothing or whatever. It just opens up a lot of doors.

What are your current projects?
Well, I just finished shooting a television series. Now I'm unemployed. Hee, hee. No—there are things in the works, but I can't talk about them. I don't want to jinx anything.

Where do you see yourself in five years?
I see myself making movies.

Any preferences as to type?
I like independent films a lot, but of course they're on a tight budget. I just basically want to make movies that are entertaining and can maybe make someone feel a certain way, change the way they think maybe for a minute or two. I don't know, I just love acting so much that I hope that in five years I will still be acting.

What do your parents think of your career?

They are very proud of me. They really are very supportive and really proud of me. They were very skeptical in the beginning. We went through a couple of difficult years, because I left home so young.

And they worried?

Very, very much! But they're great now. They're really, really proud of me, and I've turned out pretty well. They can't really complain about much. But they still give me hell about leaving home at such a young age.

Any more tips for models just starting out?

Be very confident in yourself. Never let anyone undermine you. Be yourself and look out for yourself. Be good to yourself. I think a lot of models listen to what others say—you know, it's a business where people are so critical of you all the time, and it can really affect your mind and the way you feel about yourself. Try not to let that happen, because I've seen it happen to girls, and it's really sad. To be successful you have to be secure within yourself, and you have to know yourself. You have to know your shortcomings, and you have to know what is likable and appealing about you to other people and use those things. Don't let your insecurities undermine your efforts.

What are the responsibilities of the model?

Just show up and be professional, because most likely if you're professional, that will encourage everyone else to be professional. Have a good time and don't take it too seriously, of course—we're not like saving lives here.

What about eating habits and exercise, how do you fit that in?

I always eat very light when I'm working, and when you're working three weeks straight, every day, you aren't going to have much time for exercise. And so I usually do most of my exercising when I'm not actually shooting a job.

That's how you take advantage of time you have off, you know. If you think of yourself as self-employed it's not really like you ever have a day off, because on your days off you should . . . I think as models and actresses we all think of bettering ourselves as to fitness and [our] minds.

Describe a day in your life.

When I'm working, I might have a very early call. You show up on a location or on the set very early, I would say probably between 6:00 A.M. and 9:00 A.M. You immediately go to the hair and makeup chair. You spend an hour and a half to two hours there. For an actress, you're looking over your lines the entire time. A model gets to relax. And then you go to the set and take your photos or do your scenes, basically. And there is a lot of waiting-around time in that day. And that's what causes the days to be so long. And they are usually very long days.

After that, you're completely exhausted and all you can do is go home and eat and go to sleep, you have no time to go out after. But I don't really miss a nightlife. I love my work, and I feel very fortunate to be able to do it.

14 MODEL TALK

New York's working models talk about the model lifestyle, worst modeling nightmares and dreams come true.

Maria DiAngelis

Hometown: Avondale, Pennsylvania

Years Modeling: 5

Favorite Assignment to Date
Shooting an ad campaign for a men's fragrance—I was flown first-class to a rain forest in Puerto Rico, where I met the two other models: a tame leopard and a gorgeous guy. We became great friends (the guy and I, I mean). And I made $40,000 for two days' work!

Best Thing About Modeling
Making a ton of money at a young age and still having time to go to college. I also love being self-employed. If I need a break, I can book out.

Worst Modeling Experience
We were shooting in a pool in a studio. A hose was clamped over my head and the assistants were throwing rose petals at me. By the end of the day I had swallowed a lot of water and too many rose petals.

Discovered
I was discovered in Revlon's "Unforgettable Woman" contest.

Modeling Nightmare
I caught chickenpox in Paris and couldn't work for a year because I had spots all over my face and body.

Photo: Garth Aikens

Advice to Beginning Models

Remember, it's not all about glamor. It's about business. Create an image for yourself and sell it. Forget about being young and cute. Instead, be an aggressive businesswoman and get yourself a SEPP (simplified employee pension plan).

Biggest Myth About Models

That we don't know what it's like to feel ugly.

Rhonda Niles

Hometown: Vernon, Connecticut

Years Modeling: 10

Greatest Asset as a Model
Professionalism

Favorite Assignment to Date
Cover of *Cosmopolitan* with Scavullo

Dream Assignment
Beauty (cosmetics) contract

How I Got Started as a Model
Walked into the Wilhelmina agency and asked to get started!

Strangest Modeling Story I Ever Heard

Photo: Marlena Bielinsica

The one about a top model's breast implants exploding during a transatlantic flight.

Travel Tips
Never check your luggage. Don't open a hotel room door for anybody and keep your money safe and hidden.

Angela Shelton

Hometown: Ashville, North Carolina

Years Modeling: 8

Favorite Model
Christy Turlington

Favorite Photographer
Peter Lindbergh

Favorite Designer
Dolce & Gabbana

Dream Assignment
Ten pages and the cover of *Italian Vogue* with Peter Lindbergh

Worst Modeling Experience
My agency in Paris forgot to give me my ticket for a connecting flight—had to take a taxi for four hours through Morocco at 2:00 A.M.

Health and Beauty Tips
Wash your face with Kiehl's cleanser and try your best to eat only a little ice cream.

Opinion on Cosmetic Surgery
Leave it for the housewives in Beverly Hills!

Advice to Beginning Models
Save your money. Live on a budget now and you will thank yourself a million times over ten years from now.

Biggest Myth About Models
That we're all idiots. Only some of us are!

Photo: Jon Mar

Leslie Anderson

Hometown: Pittsburgh

Years Modeling: 2

Best Thing About Modeling
The money, and meeting wonderful talented people—especially cute photographers.

Strangest Modeling Story I Ever Heard
A girl was on assignment in a third-world country. When she sat down on the toilet, a rat bit her on the butt—so the story goes.

Opinion on Plastic Surgery
Let's face it—we'd all like to have bodies like Stephanie Seymour. Well, mine doesn't look like that . . . yet!

On Life After Modeling
I'm already taking a course in fashion design and working on my own clothing line. Modeling is a wonderful opportunity for me to make all the contacts I'll need to launch a design business when I'm ready.

Angela Neil

Hometown: Mandeville, Jamaica

Years Modeling: 6

Best Modeling Job
Any job on location where we get done early and I can go sightseeing.

Worst Modeling Experience
Shooting swimwear on a beach near La Guardia Airport in December.

Health and Beauty Tip
Meditate. It focuses and relaxes you, and you'd be surprised what that does for zits!

Travel Tip
Get a good alarm clock!

Photo: Jean Gabriel Kauss

Cynthia Bailey

Hometown: Tuscumbia, Alabama

Years Modeling: 6

Favorite Model
Beverly Johnson

Favorite Photographer
Uli Rose

Favorite Designer
Isaac Mizrahi

Best Modeling Job
Doing the feature film *Without You I'm Nothing*, with Sandra Bernhard.

Advice to Beginning Models
Be your own person. Don't get influenced by the hype, drugs or promiscuity. Take your career seriously and get a financial adviser.

Strangest Modeling Story I Ever Heard
A girlfriend of mine was stalked for six months—followed from Paris to Milan to New York. It can be a danger because so many people know your face—and you don't know them.

Photo: Bolling Powell/Australian Style

Worst Thing About Modeling
You're only as good as your last tear sheet.

Afterword

I hope this book has answered some of your questions—made the world of modeling a little less mysterious. Did you realize modeling involved so much hard work and discipline? It's a business like any other. Well, maybe it's a little different. Not everyone is paid upwards of $125 per hour for their work. Not everyone has the opportunity to travel the world on assignment.

Remember that the people you meet—the models, the designers, the members of the photo crews—are like all people. They are all individuals. You can't generalize as to models. Some models are smarter than others, some more kind, less determined, more jealous, more competitive, less narcissistic, more businesslike, less caring, more intuitive, more giving—like any group of people anywhere. Maybe they fit a certain concept of physical beauty more closely than some other groups—that is probably their greatest distinction, perhaps their only distinction. So keep an open mind. You can be a model and still be yourself. And when you turn the last page and close this book, don't forget to keep learning everything you can about your business, yourself and the opportunities that surround you.

Model Credits

(in order of appearance)

Rebecca Gayheart, pp. 16, 35, 171, 172
Haley Carmouche, p. 23
Lenka, pp. 26, 27
Michele Weweje, pp. 34, 63, 152
Cynthia Bailey, pp. 35, 183
Tara Shannon, p. 36
Glenna Neece, p. 37
Kim Baker, pp. 37, 38, 129
Donna Astbury, pp. 40, 56, 57
Rachael Anne Lundblade, p. 62
Sylke, p. 64
Fiona, p. 65
Nynne, p. 66

Jay Alexander, p. 67
Pamela Dodson, p. 76
Trisha Webster, pp. 79, 80
Andre B., p. 111
Mark Vanderloo, pp. 112, 117
Michael Bergin, pp. 123, 124, 125, 126
Beverly Johnson, pp. 129, 130, 132
Tomiko, 133, 134, 135
Maria DiAngelis, p. 179
Rhonda Niles, p. 180
Angela Shelton, p. 181
Angela Neil, p. 182

Official
WILHELMINA MODEL MERCHANDISE

From Milan to Paris to the streets of New York City these products are worn and used by the male and female models of Wilhelmina. Now these products are available to you. We hope you take advantage of these special offers and we wish you the best in all of your modeling endeavors.

#034 WILHELMINA MODELS DAILY PLANNER $20
This genuine leather bound planner with the Wilhelmina Models logo embossed on the cover is an important part of every Wilhelmina model's life. From photo shoots to important appointments this daily planner is useful for scheduling appointments for anyone on the go. *Shipping/Handling $4*

#016 MODEL'S PORTFOLIO $25
If you already have tear sheets or you're just starting off, this portfolio is essential to keeping your photos organized and professional looking. The portfolio is black, hardbound and comes with ten ready-to-use pages. *Shipping/Handling $3*

#022 WILHELMINA BACKPACK $25
This black, Prada-styled backpack features the famous Wilhelmina "W" in brushed metal on the back pocket and looks great with anyone's wardrobe. Perfect for carrying a portfolio and a change of clothes for those on-the-go models. *Shipping/Handling $5*

#032 BASEBALL CAP $15
This black cap has the Wilhelmina logo on the front and the official Wilhelmina Internet address on the back. *Shipping/Handling $3*

#037 INTERNET MODEL'S T-SHIRT $15
This 100% cotton T-shirt has both the Wilhelmina logo on the front and the official Wilhelmina Internet address on the back. *(Sizes: M, L, XL. Colors: black, white) Shipping/Handling $3*

#005 MODEL'S T-SHIRT $15
This 100% cotton T-shirt has both the Wilhelmina logo on the front and back. *(Sizes: M, L, and XL. Colors: white) Shipping/Handling $3*

#035 BABY DOLL T-SHIRT $15
You've seen these tight fitted Baby Doll Tees on supermodels all over the world, now you can order the new stylish Wilhelmina Baby Doll Tee for yourself. *(Colors available: white, blue, pink, and orange. One size fits all) Shipping/Handling $3*

#036 MODEL'S WORK-OUT TANK TOP $15
Whether you're at the gym or just hanging out, this work-out tank top is sharp, with the Wilhelmina "W" on the front and the official Wilhelmina Internet address on the back. *(Sizes: M, L, XL. Colors: athletic grey, white) Shipping/Handling $3*

#033 WILHELMINA BOMBER JACKET $225
This lined, all black, wool jacket with genuine leather sleeves is hot and is perfect for just about any season. The official Wilhelmina logos have been embroidered on the front and back along with a special "W" patch on the sleeve. *(Sizes: M, L, XL) Shipping/Handling $10*

To order please call
(800) 889-MODEL
Or send a check or money order payable to Wilhelmina Model Merchandise,
at 300 Park Avenue South, 2nd Floor, New York, NY 10010.

WILHELMINA

MODEL SEARCH

GRAND PRIZE:

$100,000

MODELING CONTRACT WITH WILHELMINA MODELS

Age: 13 years old and above
Sex: Female

Wilhelmina Model Search is open to all women ages 13 and above. If you would like to receive more information on entering the annual model search or becoming a Wilhelmina model and the winner of the $100,000 contract, complete the entry form request below or call (212) 477-3112.

Good luck with your modeling endeavors.

ENTRY FORM REQUEST

- -

FIRST NAME   LAST NAME

ADDRESS   APT. #

CITY   STATE   ZIP

TELEPHONE   CODE

/   /   **SS**

D.O.B

Note: Do not send in photograph(s) now. Wait to receive entry form.

MAIL TO:

**WILHELMINA MODEL SEARCH/ SS REQUEST • 300 PARK AVENUE SOUTH • 2ND FLOOR
NEW YORK • NY • 10010 OR CALL (212) 477-3112**

Printed in the United States
134619LV00002B/1/P

9 780684 814919